christian grandparenting network

# courageous
# grandparenting

## unshakable faith in a broken world

## cavin harper

published by
the christian grandparenting network
colorado springs, colorado

Cavin Harper is every grandparent's "new best friend!"
**Courageous Grandparenting** is filled with all the right stuff—
stories and statistics, ideas and ideals, humor and hopefulness.
He lays out the power of words and blessings and shows us
how we can offer them up as sacred gifts.
With a strong reminder that "we're not in Kansas anymore,"
he helps us share values and virtues with the ones who
want to hear from the gray champions in their lives.
Thanks, Cavin, for a timely epistle and a great read!

Dr. Ward Tanneberg, President/Executive Director, The CASA Network

## COURAGEOUS GRANDPARENTING

**Copyright © 2013 Cavin T. Harper**

Published by the Christian Grandparenting Network, a ministry of ElderQuest Ministries
5844 Pioneer Mesa Dr
Colorado Springs, CO 80923

Unless otherwise noted, Scripture quotations are from THE HOLY BIBLE, NEW INTERNATIONAL VERSION®, NIV® Copyright © 1973, 1978, 1984, 2011 by Biblica, Inc.™ Used by permission. All rights reserved worldwide.

Scripture quotations taken from the New American Standard Bible®, Copyright © 1960, 1962, 1963, 1968, 1971, 1972, 1973, 1975, 1977, 1995 by The Lockman Foundation. Used by permission. (www.Lockman.org)

Scripture quotations from *The Message*. Copyright © Eugene H. Peterson, 1993, 1994, 1995, 1996, 2000, 2001, 2002. Used by permission of NavPress Publishing Group. All rights reserved.

Scripture quotations marked (GNT) are from the Good News Translation in Today's English Version- Second Edition Copyright © 1992 by American Bible Society. Used by Permission.

Scripture quotations marked (NLT) are taken from the Holy Bible, New Living Translation, copyright © 1996, 2004, 2007 by Tyndale House Foundation. Used by permission of Tyndale House Publishers, Inc., Carol Stream, Illinois 60188. All rights reserved.

Italics used in Scripture quotations have been added by the author for emphasis.

## ISBN 978-1-4675-1316-6

© 2012 Cavin T. Harper

Cover Design by Chuck Haas; Colorado Springs, CO
Printed in the United States by Snowfall Press, Monument, CO
First Edition 2012 (*Formerly Titled: Not On Our Watch!*)
Revised Edition 2013

# courageous
# grandparenting

**Courageous Grandparenting** challenges grandparents to sense the urgency of these turbulent times, participate in their grandchildren's worlds, and maximize opportunities to credibly, creatively engage them. With passion and practical advice, **Courageous Grandparenting** offers the reader dozens of activities to help guide grandchildren through life with faith and integrity. Cavin asks,"What might God do through the lives of millions of radical grandparents if they choose to resolutely stand upon an unshakable faith in God and the Gospel?" Here is an invitation to join him and other grandparents who share a passion to invest their lives in radical grandparenting for such a time as this.

Linda Thomas, Author, *Grandma's Letters from Africa*, www.grandmaslettersfromafrica.blogspot.com

This book has caused me to look at my grandparenting style to a degree that I never have before. I am not an uninvolved grandparent. In fact I think of myself as a pretty good one. For years I've known that all our grandchildren are at risk of losing everything, even their very souls. But now our tumultuous culture is at the apex of its very tipping point. And I've taken a too-easy road in the past. That changes-right now! My grandchildren are one of God's most important gifts. Cavin aptly and passionately says, "There's a battle raging for the hearts and minds of our grandchildren. The enemy is intent on destroying their souls. God's grand call is for grandparents to engage that enemy and fight for their souls." I'm now absolutely convinced that's what *courageous, radically loving grandparents must do*. My full armor is now on. I will not give up one more inch or moment being passive about what is my most important role in my grandchildren's lives. I urge you to read this important book. Then act upon its critical and timely message. Your grandchildren's lives depend on it. And time is running out!

Jane Terry, President TresMark Communications; Denver, CO

Cavin Harper has issued an urgent call for courageous grandparenting in the turbulent times we live in today. He compares this call to Nehemiah's call to rebuild the temple and fight for the faith for our families. Baby Boomer grandparents and beyond are urged to wake up, wise up, and rise up to their God given responsibility. Christian grandparents have a sacred trust to co-partner with God to pass His faithfulness on to their future generations. As a result of reading this book, you will gain a fresh view of what it means to be an intentional, radical Christian grandparent for our time.

Lillian Penner, National Prayer Coordinator for Christian Grandparenting Network;
Author of *Grandparenting with a Purpose*

**Courageous Grandparenting** is a "must read" for every Christian grandparent who wants to make a difference in the lives of their grandchildren. Cavin's intentional, relevant, motivating approach with common sense suggestions will make you wonder why you haven't been doing those things from the day you first knew a "little one" was going to join your family. This book will forever change the way you view your responsibilities as a grandparent.

Lana Rockwell, author of *Passing On A Written Legacy*, www.mymemoriesforyou.net

**Courageous Grandparenting** provides a loving "kick-in-the-behind" motivation to inspire today's grandparents to make the most of their grandparenting season by passing along their wisdom, faith, and legacy to the generations that follow. This book is for grandparents everywhere who want their Golden Years to count for eternity.

Renée Gray-Wilburn, co-author, *Grandparenting Through Obstacles: Overcoming Family Challenges to Reach Your Grandchildren for Christ*

# acknowledgments

To the greatest, most creative, grandmother I know, my BFF and love of my life, Diane, affectionately known as Nana by her adoring grandchildren; to my two beautiful daughters, Laura and Alisa, two amazing and courageous mothers; and to my grandchildren, Thomas, Wesley, Corban, Daniel, Annalisa, Courtney, Jonathan and our newest arrival, Joshua. You are my inspiration for this book and the reason I love being a grandfather. May you know the One who is my all-satisfying delight, and may He be yours as well. There is no greater gift your Nana and I could leave to you than that Jesus is your anchor in life, *fastened to the Rock that cannot move; grounded firm and deep in the Savior's love.*

These are some of the special friends who helped make this project possible. Their input and critiques kept me focused and resulted in new directions I had not even considered. I cannot thank enough my wife, Diane, who patiently endured with me and exhorted me along the way. A special thanks also to Reneé Gray-Wilburn who was my editor and gave me some great advice along the way.

Judy Marie Carlson
Jane Terry
Tom and Terri Streelman
Paul and Dianna Miller
Bryan Haynes
Linda Thomas
Lillian Penner
Chuck Haas
Stan and Penny Russell

When all is said and done, it is my hope that what is written in these pages can only be expressed thus: Soli Deo Gloria!

# table of contents

# preface

g r a n d p a u s e :
*"I have no greater joy than to hear that my children walk in truth"*
3 John 1:4

I heard the light *tap, tap, tap* on my study door. "Now who could that be this early in the morning?" I whispered loud enough to be heard. Slowly the door creaked open. At the sight of my smile, a grinning ball of energy burst in my office. I laughed as my ten-year-old grandson leapt into my lap, wrapped his arms around my neck, and squeezed. I squeezed back. No words were required in those few moments of embraceable delight that had become a frequent morning ritual in our home. I hope he never tires of the ritual. I know I never will.

I love being a grandfather. I enjoy being called 'Papa' and doing crazy things with my grandkids. As much as I enjoy the perks that come with being a grandparent, I have no desire to sit around and simply be a *good* grandfather. I am not content to be nothing more than a good time for my grandkids. I want to live as courageously and intentionally as I can so they will understand the Gospel and choose to walk in the truth.

I don't want to be found guilty of trivializing or neglecting my responsibility as a 'Keeper of the Spring' (see Introduction). I don't want to be a barn-builder; I want to be a legacy-builder—the kind of legacy my grandkids will want to embrace and will outlive me for generations after me. I want them to see the glory, the goodness, the grace, and the greatness of God in me, and I want them to want it for themselves.

Whenever I watch network news or listen to talk radio or read a newspaper, it seems obvious to me that we have not created a brave new world, but a broken, aimless world. Have you ever thought about that? It's time to stop our self-absorbed lives long enough to consider the consequences of the mess we are leaving for the next generations.

There is no doubt that evil times are nothing new in human history. Yet, there is something alarming about much of today's research that suggests a *black hole* of missing-in-action young adults who want nothing to do with Christianity or the church.

I recently picked up a copy of *You Lost Me*, written by David Kinnaman, president of the Barna Group. Calling attention to this unusual 'black hole' today, he writes, "If you're an older believer, a parent, or a Christian leader, I am not pointing the finger of blame at you. Instead, I want us to recognize together our collective calling to love, accept, and partner with this next generation. That's not easy…we have to admit that we have messed up too often, attempted the impossible by our own effort, and missed divine moments of opportunity. *But we don't have to miss the next ones (italics mine)*."[1]

Kinnaman is right…we don't have to miss the next ones, but we will if we are not courageous and intentional about our responsibility before God. When I originally wrote this book, it was entitled *Not On Our Watch: Courageous Grandparenting in a Turbulent World.* In it I laid out some specific ways grandparents can build a legacy that outlives them. My intent was to challenge grandparents to take seriously their responsibility to tell the next generations the truth about God and the Gospel of Jesus Christ. We are, as Dr. John Piper explains it[2], to live our lives making much of Christ in our lives as our all-satisfying delight so that our children and grandchildren will know the truth and desire to walk in it as well. There is no greater joy for a parent or grandparent than to see their children walk in the truth.

The fact is we have messed up on numerous fronts. So, the question is, are we willing step back long enough to see the big picture and what it means for the next generations? Are we able to see the sin that has led to the condition of the world we helped create, and own it as our sin?

Some will deny the problem is theirs. Some will seek to blame others. Neither approach offers an interest in solutions. Those who own up to their sin, repent, and surrender to God's grace and power to fight for their families, become conduits of hope for this generation. They will open the door for God to do more than we could ever imagine for His glory.

Something similar appears to have happened in Joshua's time as well. After he and all those amazing leaders who led the conquest of the Promised Land died, somehow the generations after them did not know or follow the Lord. How did that happen? When I look at my generation, I can't help but wonder if history may, in fact, be repeating itself.

I will confess that I'm not a perfect grandparent. I make some of the same mistakes as a grandparent that I made as a parent. I often question what I'm doing writing this book and directing the Christian Grandparenting Network. I have more than my share of messed-up issues in my life and family. I feel the angst Moses must have felt when God asked him to be His spokesman in Egypt. I understand Moses' hesitance. Why would anyone listen to me, Lord, since I speak with faltering lips as well?

For purposes only God knows, He has not released me from the assignment He gave me. In spite of my limitations, I am compelled to stay the course, determined to learn from my mistakes, and driven to call upon others to join the cause. There is one thing I am resolved not to do. I will not let my grandchildren grow up not knowing Christ and what God has done for me on my watch! I will not become a deadbeat granddad who fails to speak the truth in love.

If you are a grandparent, you know that few things in life compare to it. Still, as *grand* as grandparenting is, there are days when it doesn't feel so grand. I'm not so naïve to believe that grandparenting is always filled with moments like those when my grandson bursts into my study. The dreams we hold for our families are not always fulfilled. For many of you, being a grandparent means living with mountains of heartache, discouragement, and disappointment. I pray that this book will give you hope and strengthen you so you do not lose heart.

I believe that most grandparents have a deep longing to play a meaningful role in their grandchildren's life story. Most parents I know also want that as well. That's my motivation for writing this book. My hope is that when you have finished reading, you will know that you have the necessary tools to help you play out your role successfully—as Heaven measures success. But make no mistake…the hearts and souls of our grandchildren are at stake. It is not enough to be convicted. There must be a sense of urgency to compel us to dare to die to self and our agendas. Only then will we dare to live the life we were meant to live—life with a capital 'L.'

Courageous, godly parents and grandparents share a passionate commitment to do everything they can to help the next generations know Christ and wholeheartedly follow Him as Lord and Savior. They are not content to settle for the easy road. They want to make Christ look great in the eyes of the next generations. This book will unpack what that looks like in today's world.

Builder and Boomer generations represent the majority of today's grandparents. There are nearly eighty million of us. Yet, on our watch we have stood by in silence and allowed the Father of Lies to inject his venom into our culture, hardening men's hearts to the truth. The world we have left for the next generation to inherit is filled with darkness, turbulence, and uncertainty. That's the bad news.

The good news is that these are also times of extraordinary opportunity. Courageous believers who display an unshakable belief in the gospel and in God's Word marked by compassion, authenticity, and humility, will witness God do a radical thing in our world. Your grandchildren don't need *good* grandparents. They need and deserve *intentional* grandparents (and parents)—those who dare to embrace God's purposes for their sake.

If you have picked up this book because you are looking for more tips about how to enjoy your grandkids or be their BFF (texting lingo for *best friends forever*), you will be disappointed. Having determined to do all I can by God's power to keep my grandchildren from becoming casualties of the lies of this world on my watch, I have learned that I cannot do it alone. This is a community affair; a generational responsibility.

I believe the Church is the hope of the world. It is God's tool through which all the generations experience and display the glory, the goodness, the grace and the greatness of God for the world to see. According to Scripture, such a display of God's glory happens when "the *whole body, joined and held together by every supporting ligament, grows and builds itself up in love, as each part does its work*" *(Eph. 4:16)*. This is how the body of Christ—the family of God—was designed to function. It is our collective calling.

*Courageous Grandparenting* is an invitation for you to join me in a cause that is bigger than all of us. Together, we can directly impact the eternal destiny of another generation. We cannot afford to waste our lives. It is time to seize the moment and live wisely while there is still time.

But let's be honest with one another. This will not be an easy journey. The opposition is intense and relentless. The task can seem overwhelming and daunting. Nehemiah faced his share of opposition when he arrived in Jerusalem to rebuild the wall. We will draw from his courageous journey of faith to guide us in our mission to rebuild the walls of truth that lie in ruins today. It will be a journey that is undeniably dangerous. There are no guarantees of the outcome. On the other hand, what could be more dangerous than sitting back, getting comfortable, and doing nothing to rescue those who are perishing on our watch?

~Cavin T. Harper

# introduction
## a   p a r a b l e

Life is often not what it seems. In the village of Fairwater life couldn't be any better—or so it seemed. Fairwater's story is our story. It's about ordinary people, like you and me, who live every day with few expectations that things could ever be anything but good.

Nestled at the northern edge of a lush mountain valley accented by dazzling displays of colorful alpine flora the village of Fairwater sat in all its glory. Its grassy meadows and jeweled landscape were bordered by towering snow-capped mountains that stood like stately sentinels keeping watch over a magical panorama of beauty and majesty.

High in these magnificent mountains lived a kind and hospitable hermit by the name of Josef. Josef was the Keeper of the Spring for Fairwater. His job was to maintain the wellspring that generously supplied the village's most precious commodity and source of its prosperity—its water. Though faithful in the performance of his duties, he had done it for so long than anyone who still knew of him could remember.

The spring produced deliciously sweet and refreshing water unlike any other in the region. Vacationers, health seekers, fishermen and merchants came from throughout the kingdom to savor Fairwater's delicious water. Many believed the water possessed healing powers. Visitors arrived daily to fill bottles and jars with the invigorating liquid pouring from the enormous public fountain in the center of town.

Children rollicked in the clear pools in the village and nearby Crystal Lake where fisherman found some of the best fishing imaginable. It would not be inaccurate to say that in Fairwater one could find a part of the world where life may simply be described as *good*.

Josef rarely wandered far from the spring and cottage in which he lived. In fact, he had not been to the village for years, which explains why most people in Fairwater forgot he even existed. The few who remembered knew him only as an old hermit living by himself in the hills. Few knew what he did up there.

It's not difficult to understand why. The stories about the history of the wellspring that once passed from generation to generation gradually ceased being told altogether. A long life of ease and contentment in their peaceful valley gradually erased all recollection of the stories from the community memory. The good life of Fairwater was simply taken for granted.

It was inevitable, I suppose, that the village would question the need for a Keeper of the Spring. The Fairwater town council no longer had members who remembered anything about Josef and his duties. A diligent council would after all not keep something in its budget that was unnecessary. So, the decision was made to terminate the single line item simply listed as "Spring Keeper."

It was equally inevitable, I suppose, that an inner restlessness would find its way into Josef's heart. After all, the stories he heard from occasional travelers who came by his mountain cottage had stirred a desire to explore the world they described outside the valley—places he could only imagine.

So, when the notice arrived that his position had been terminated, though there was a bit of sadness at leaving all that he had ever know, a new excitement emerged at the prospects of a new adventure in his life.

Still he wondered who would take care of the Spring. *I guess they'll have to figure it out on their own*, he shrugged. With that, he packed his few belongings, locked up the cottage, and set out to experience life beyond the spring.

Things in Fairwater continued much as they always had…for a while. Gradually, however, subtle changes occurred at the wellspring of which no one in the village was aware. Piles of rotting pine needles and other decaying forest vegetation steadily built up around the spring. Trash left by the occasional travelers accumulated around the cottage and wellspring. For a time the flow from the spring was strong enough to break through the accumulating debris and force its way into the stream channel.

Over the next two years, however, things changed noticeably. The natural buildup owing to the cycles of nature caused the unremitting stream to ever so slowly surrender to the build up around the well. With the stream channel blocked, the water gradually dispersed around the cottage creating a marshy bog.

In the village people noticed that the water flowing into the pools and fountain had slowed. A peculiar greenish tint in the water was observed as well. Several voiced their concern to the Village Council.

"We assure you it's nothing", the Council responded. "We still have the purest water in the region. There's nothing to worry about. We're sure this is just a temporary situation. We have our best people looking into it. Everything will be fine."

In spite of their assurances, it was not long before a number of children in the village began to complain of intense stomach pain. Some became so ill they had to stay home from school. Before long, most of the village children were sick. Doctors diagnosed it as some kind of virus, perhaps brought in by outsiders. Confident it would run its course in a few weeks, they prescribed rest and yes… drink lots of water.

Before long things went from bad to worse. Not only were the children getting sicker, a few died from their illness. Adults were not immune either, particularly the elderly. Panic surged through the village. People demanded answers. The Council tried to assure them everything was under control, insisting it would soon run its course and everything would be back to normal.

It did run its course—but not as predicted. By the end of the second year all the water in the village revealed an obvious green hue and emitted a putrid, rotten odor. Dead fish were spotted along the shoreline of their once popular lake. The level in the lake dropped dramatically making it more of a swamp than the pristine fishing destination it had once been.

Fisherman stopped coming to Fairwater. Tourists no longer came to the village to swim in the pools or buy bottles of the famous water. Outsiders began to call Fairwater, *Foulwater*. The village was dying, and no one knew what to do to save it. In spite of all of this, the Council continued to assert that everything would be fine.

Their patience exhausted, the villagers called for an emergency Council meeting. Tempers flared, as people demanded truthful answers. As accusations flew around the room, no one noticed the stranger quietly slip into the room and take a seat in the back. As the hostility escalated, the stranger finally rose to his feet and asked to address the Council.

"I know the source of your problem and how to fix it," he said.

"*You* know how to fix it?" scoffed one councilman. "You know more than all of the experts who have been working on this for nearly two years?"

"Perhaps I do," the stranger replied.

"Is that so. So, you are a hydrologist, then?"

"I don't know what that is, but I do…"

"I see. Sir, I don't know who you are, but I thank you for your concern. This is a matter that demands trained experts to resolve. I think we will manage just fine without your help."

"So it appears," the old man replied. Some of the villagers chuckled at the old man's comment.

"If I may be so bold, I'm not one of those fancy-titled experts you mentioned—hydro…whatever, but I do know the cause of the problem and how to fix it…if you're interested."

Before the Council could respond, one of the villagers jumped to his feet. "We want to hear what he has to say. You keep promising us solutions, but nothing improves. It only gets worse. What have we got to lose? Let him speak!"

The rest of the crowd shouted their support, so the Council was forced to relent. They granted him five minutes to say what he had to say.

"The problem is simple and so is the solution," he began. "The problem and the solution both relate to a decision this Council made two years ago to eliminate a vital position for the benefit of this village. You must restore the position of Keeper of the Spring."

"The what?" a councilman asked.

"Have you forgotten so soon? The Keeper of the Spring has been an essential part of this community since its beginning," the stranger continued, "but the Council decided two years ago that it was an unnecessary cost. Had they done their research, they would have discovered that long ago the founders of this village considered it important enough to secure the King's royal sanction. The Keeper's absence is why the water is bad and why the children and the village suffer. Reinstate the Keeper of the Spring and Fairwater will soon be rid of its foul water."

The room reverberated with the murmurs of people trying to make sense of what the stranger said. A handful of people mentioned distant memories of stories about a Keeper of some kind, but no one could remember anything more.

The Clerk of the Council immediately searched the old records of Fairwater and found the record of the royal decree. He read it aloud as everyone listened attentively. When he finished, silence sat like a mist over the room for several moments.

Finally, the Council President stood and apologized to the villagers for having neglected something of such importance. He immediately called for a vote to reinstate the position of Keeper of the Spring in Fairwater. Loud cheers rose from the villagers as the vote passed unanimously.

Once again, the stranger stood and asked to speak. "I must be truthful with you. The Council is only partly to blame for this mess. I am ashamed to admit that I am also to blame."

A low rumble echoed in the chamber as the stranger continued. "My name is Josef. I may be a stranger to you, but I was the Keeper of the Spring for a very long time…at least until I foolishly allowed the Council to make this decision without trying to convince them otherwise. You see, I thought I had earned the right to do more important things. I convinced myself that I'd done my duty, that I was under appreciated, and that I deserved a chance to do what I always dreamed of doing—seeing the world.

"The truth is that I neglected my duty to this village. Over the years I isolated myself from you and failed to keep the stories and history of Fairwater alive so the Council would know how important the Keeper of the Spring is to this community. My silent abdication of responsibility to you and your children allowed the story that is so vital to you to fade from our community memory on my watch.

"I realize what a fool I have been. I ask your forgiveness for my foolishness. I abandoned my responsibility and pursued a meaningless quest at the expense of your children and all the residents of Fairwater. I was so focused on myself that I failed to warn the Council about the risks involved. I ask your forgiveness. I wish I could undo the damage that has been done."

As Josef started to leave, one of the villagers stopped him and said, "Sir, I don't think you should bear all the responsibility for our condition. All of us in this room are guilty of allowing the story of the Keeper be forgotten. We share the blame. We need you, Josef, to be our Keeper of the Spring once again, but with one condition. You must agree to form an apprenticeship school to train future Keepers of the Spring. We must ensure that the King's service for this village will continue for generations to come. And…I propose that the history of Fairwater and the Keeper of the Spring be required instruction in our schools. You are the best person to help us tell the story."

Within months after the Council's decision to reinstate Josef as Keeper of the Spring, life in Fairwater improved dramatically. The pools and fountains ran clear and pure once again. The health of the community improved noticeably once the pools and fountain had been cleansed with fresh water from the spring. Eventually the lake recaptured its reputation as a fisherman's paradise—much to everyone's delight. Once again life in Fairwater was good because the Keeper of the Spring was on duty.

I wish I could say our story ends here. Unfortunately, while clean water once again graced Fairwater's pools and fountains, the damage from protracted neglect would be felt in the village for many years to come. The grief of personal losses already suffered could not be assuaged. The long-term effects of drinking polluted water would serve as a constant reminder of the reality of neglect, complacency and ignorance.

For Josef, his brief 'retirement' became a painful reminder of the consequences of selfish decisions. Fortunately, he learned that none of the allurements of the world could substitute for being a conduit of life and blessing to others. He also discovered that being unnoticed did not diminish a person's value or responsibility. The good news is that Josef learned that with only one life to live, it wasn't worth it to waste it living only for himself.

Most of all, he learned that forgetting who he is and why he is here impacts many more lives than just his own. Neglecting responsibility allows the filth of the world to strangle the flow of blessing and hope for the next generations. Josef resolved to never let that happen on his watch again.

What about our story? Who is tending the wellspring of our nation, of our communities, of our families? Does it smell to you like something's in the water? It's time to wake up and clean the spring.

## p a r t   o n e

# WAKE UP!

*The memoirs of Nehemiah, son of Hacaliah.*

*It was the month of Kislev in the twentieth year. At the time I was in the palace complex at Susa. Hanani, one of my brothers, had just arrived from Judah with some fellow Jews. I asked them about the conditions among the Jews there who had survived the exile, and about Jerusalem.*

*They told me, "The exile survivors who are left there in the province are in bad shape. Conditions are appalling. The wall of Jerusalem is still rubble; the city gates are still cinders."*

*When I heard this, I sat down and wept. I mourned for days, fasting and praying before the God of Heaven.*

*I said, "God, God of Heaven, the great and awesome God, loyal to his covenant and faithful to those who love him and obey his commands: Look at me, listen to me. Pay attention to this prayer of your servant that I'm praying day and night in intercession for your servants, the people of Israel, confessing the sins of the People of Israel. And I'm including myself, I and my ancestors, among those who have sinned against you.*

*"We've treated you like dirt: We haven't done what you told us, haven't followed your commands, and haven't respected the decisions you gave to Moses your servant. All the same, remember the warning you posted to your servant Moses: 'If you betray me, I'll scatter you to the four winds, but if you come back to me and do what I tell you, I'll gather up all these scattered peoples from wherever they ended up and put them back in the place I chose to mark with my Name.'"*

*…The king then asked me, "So what do you want?"*

*Praying under my breath to the God of Heaven, I said, "If it please the king, and if the king thinks well of me, send me to Judah, to the city where my family is buried, so that I can rebuild it…"*

*So I arrived in Jerusalem…then I gave them my report: "Face it: we're in a bad way here. Jerusalem is a wreck; its gates are burned up. Come—let's build the wall of Jerusalem and not live with this disgrace any longer."*

Excerpts from Nehemiah, chapters 1 & 2 (The Message)

# not on my watch!

g r a n d p a u s e :

*"He who disregards his calling will never keep the straight path in the duties of his work."*

John Calvin

**M**y wife and I drove the two hours to the hospital after receiving the call from our son-in-law. We arrived and rushed to the room where our daughter Alisa was about to give birth to our first grandchild. Two weeks shy of my forty-ninth birthday my first grandchild was on the way, and I was going to be there to experience it all—well, at least the final outcome.

As the paternal grandfather and I sat in the waiting room across the hall, my wife, Diane, soon walked in to deliver the news—we had a grandson, Thomas Granville Lane. In spite of some complications with his breathing, she informed us that our blue baby would be okay.

Gratefully, Thomas' Avatar-like blue tint soon turned to a healthy pink complexion. Now that he is a teenager, I sometimes tease him about his oxygen deficiency at birth. "It explains so much about you today," I tell him. He just grins and rolls his eyes.

I don't know about you, but something happened to me that day when Thomas entered our world. I experienced a wave of indescribable exhilaration. At the same time I felt an undeniable horror at the realization that I was old enough to be a grandfather. How did that happen? I don't remember seeing any gray hair when I looked in the mirror that morning. Did I miss something along the way?

If you're a grandparent you understand. Undoubtedly you've experienced that same incredible rush when your first grandchild arrives, only to be startled by the sober reality that you are a one of *them*—a grandparent.

Fortunately for us, that brutal reality check represented by the number of candles on our birthday cake is mostly overridden by the inexpressible delight of being inducted into that elite club reserved for grandparents. It doesn't get any better than this. As special as that first grandchild is, the successive arrival of each additional grandchild continues to be a grand moment as well.

## who's telling the story?

My life was changed that day my first grandchild arrived on the scene. It involved more than an age awakening or the blessing of witnessing a new generation arrive on the scene. A different sort of awakening changed my life that day.

Shortly before Thomas was born I was reading in the book of Judges. As I held my first grandchild in that hospital nursery and gazed into his cherub-like face, an unsettling sensation invaded my soul. The words of Judges 2:10 churned in my mind: *"After that whole generation (Joshua's generation) had been gathered to their fathers, **another generation grew up, who knew neither the Lord nor what He had done for Israel"** (emphasis mine).*

Think about it—how is it that the generation after Joshua lost the stories about the miracles God had performed to bring them to the Promised Land? Were they asleep when the stories were being told? Perhaps their parents were too tired after a week of marching around the walls of Jericho to take the time to tell them. It's difficult for me to imagine how these amazing adventures were not being told and re-told almost every night around the tribal bonfires. Where did the ball get dropped? How could they not know the stories when they were that close to all the action? Why weren't the *spring-keepers* making sure that the truth about God's faithfulness and greatness flowed to the next generations?

The Bible doesn't tell us what happened, only that they did not know. All we know for sure is that another generation grew up and rejected the faith of their fathers. It's a pattern that has been repeated among God's people throughout history. Now it has raised its ugly head once again in our time.

I was unable to evade the trouble in my soul that June day in 1997 as I held my grandson. It struck me that what had happened in Joshua's day could happen in mine. I prayed…*Lord, may those words in Judges 2 never be the epitaph of my life or my generation. I do not want to fail to show Your greatness to this grandchild or any other grandchild You may give us. May it never be said of my grandson or his generation, Lord, that they grew up not hearing about You on my watch!*

That day I determined to make sure my grandchildren knew the story. Even more, I wanted to do all I could to make sure my generation of emerging grandparents understood what was at stake if we did not wake up to our responsibility. We cannot afford to let the next generations miss the importance of God's grace and greatness on our watch!

Your part in the story that God is writing for your grandchildren is critical. Behind God's instructions to tell the next generations are the dual realities of purpose and urgency. God has carved out a very specific role for you to play in His story. You are His conduit of blessing in your grandchildren's lives. This is more than one person's or one family's story. It's a legacy of faith and hope about *God's story* written from one generation to another. It's a legacy that gives them assurance to never have reason to think of themselves as unloved or unblessed.

# a grand call

Grandparenting is a grand call—a divine call, if I understand it correctly, that must not be wasted.

A certain man discovered a canvas bag full of hardened clay balls while exploring a cave along the seashore. About the size of his fist, they appeared to be of little worth to anyone. He surmised that they must be the handiwork of children playing on the beach. Perhaps, after the clay balls baked in the sun, they placed them in the canvas bag, carried them to the cave to play, and forgot about them.

Snatching the bag of clay balls, the man continued on his way down the beach. As he walked along the shore he reached in the bag and amused himself by tossing them, one at a time, as far out into the ocean as he could. He had launched about half the clay balls when one accidentally dropped from his hand as he pulled it from the bag. The ball fell against rocks on the shore and cracked open. He couldn't believe his eyes. Stooping down to look more closely, he discovered a precious gem encased inside—a treasure in the clay.

He quickly broke open the remaining balls. Each one contained what turned out to be a rare, very valuable gem. He held a fortune in his hands. Instantly the color drained from his face as he visualized all the balls he had foolishly thrown into the ocean—lost forever.

I have to admit that, as a grandfather, I loved rolling on the floor with my grandkids when they were young. Those were special moments as they crawled all over me squealing and laughing. However, if enjoying my grandkids and doing fun things is the only trophy I have on the mantle, then I've missed the call. Like the man throwing away the valuable gems I could easily throw away precious opportunities to point my grandchildren toward the truth. I mustn't let that happen—not on my watch.

In my grandparents' home a plaque once hung. It contained a poem by C. T. Studd:

> *Only one life*
> *'Twill soon be past;*
> *Only what's done*
> *For Christ will last.*[1]

What comes to your mind when you consider how you've lived your life? Do you ever feel that pang of guilt about what has been wasted—tossed into the ocean like those clay balls never to be recovered?  Some might legitimately argue that contemplating such things is a fool's errand—the kind that led George Bailey to jump off a bridge in the Christmas classic, *It's A Wonderful Life*. Some will say there is no point to entertaining thoughts about what could have been? It serves no useful purpose. I disagree.

An honest evaluation of how you're living your life is a healthy process. Knowing you only have one life to live can force you to ask whether you are living your life as God intends it to be lived or not. Like treasures in clay, what is thrown away may no longer be recovered. Unless you understand the significance of lost opportunities, the cleansing power of repentance, and what it means to be God's workmanship, you will be prone to wasteful living.

Another of America's film classics is *The Wizard of Oz*. The story transports us from ordinary black-and-white scenes to dazzling full-color landscapes as we follow the strange adventures of a young girl named Dorothy. Caught in a severe storm, Dorothy and her little dog, Toto, are swept away in the family farmhouse by a tornado and deposited into the magical world of Oz. As they step from the farmhouse and look around, Dorothy makes the memorable statement, "Toto, I've a feeling we're not in Kansas anymore."

For those of us born more than fifty years ago, today's world feels very different from the one in which we grew up. Like the explosion from black and white to Technicolor, much has changed in a short time, and continues to do so. Postmodernism, technology, global terrorism, and more have reshaped our world and our culture dramatically. Like it or not, we're not in Kansas anymore.

Step out of your own world, and take a look at the world around you. There is no wicked witch, but there is a pile of rubble of wickedness and rebellion. If you search through the rubble, you'll find broken families, hopelessness, and a nation who has forgotten its roots. The walls are crumbled and the gates are burned. But what can we do? We can get angry and complain, or we could choose to follow Nehemiah's example.

## first things first

The story of Nehemiah is our scriptural sextant for navigating the turbulent seas of life as vessels of God's grace and truth. Here was a man who was not about to let his circumstances keep him from taking action—not when his homeland lay in ruins. He could not bear the thought of letting that which had been the symbol of God's glory and faithfulness remain a pile of rubble.

Notice his response when awakened to the condition of Jerusalem: *"When I heard this, I sat down and wept. I mourned for days, fasting and praying before the God of Heaven"* (Nehemiah 1:4). Did you catch that? He wept. His heart was broken over the condition of his homeland. When was the last time you wept over the condition of our homeland?

Nehemiah's weeping led him to fasting and praying. Here's what he prayed: *"I confess the sins we Israelites, including myself and my father's house, have committed against you. We have acted very wickedly against you. We have not obeyed the command, decrees and law you gave your servant Moses"* (Nehemiah 1:6)

On his knees before the God of Heaven, he confessed his own sin and that of his people. Hold on a moment! Why would Nehemiah repent for something that was not his doing? This was another generation's problem, right? Nehemiah's understanding of sin and God's holiness led him to quite a different conclusion. This was his sin too. He understood that without a repentant heart the cycle would continue.

Have you noticed how repentance is not a much-talked about or practiced posture in America today, including the church? Why is that? I suggest it has to do with how we view God. We are bombarded with talk of God's love and grace, but hear little about fearing God. We like the idea of being forgiven and how God will love us regardless of our mistakes. Repentance is little more than feeling sorry for doing something wrong. But repentance, true repentance, is a turning completely away from the horrible affront our self-centeredness, our self-righteousness, and our self-esteem is to the glory, goodness, greatness and holiness of God.

We read stories of great men of old, like Nehemiah, and fail to see the application to our own lives. Nehemiah had an important position serving an earthly king with great power. He was still a slave working for a king who had the power to take his life for any reason. Yet he knew this king was nothing in comparison to the King of all Creation, who held both his life and his soul in His hand. Knowing this holy God meant he also knew himself. How could he not repent for his own sin and the sins of his people?

It was this repentant heart that freed him to be a vessel in God's hands. He knew his God was not only just, but merciful and that his promise to forgive and restore was not like the promises of fickle human kings or presidents. Nehemiah did not pray that someone else would catch the vision to repair the city walls. He knew that he must assume responsibility, even though he was an exile in Babylon. He also knew only God could give him success to complete what God had laid on his heart.

Paul wrote to the church in Ephesus reminding them (and us) that *"we are God's workmanship created in Christ Jesus to do good works which God prepared in advance for us to do"* (Ephesians 2:10). Did you catch that? We are *God's* workmanship. We are not masters of our fate or captains of our souls. If we think so, we may soon find ourselves in the embarrassing position of having steered our ship onto the rocks—if we haven't already.

Nehemiah understood the *workmanship principle* hundreds of years before Paul labeled it. He wasn't worried about whether this assignment was part of his gift mix or not. He did not toss the matter aside as somebody else's problem.

His comfortable position in the king's court did not keep him from taking on something that would take him outside his comfort zone.

Nehemiah's heart was broken by the news of his hometown's condition. He never questioned whether he should do something. He knew the only obstacle would be an unrepentant heart. He believed the promise God made if His people would repent and turn their hearts back to Him. Upon that promise he surrendered himself completely. This was God's work. He was simply responding to His call to go and see the great wonders God had yet to perform.

There are special purposes for which God calls particular people. At the same time God calls *all* of us to rise up and take on the battle. Our families, our homes, our nation lay in ruins. There are walls that need rebuilding in our own nation. We can pretend everything is fine or that it's not our problem. Ignorance is not bliss in this situation. Neither is complacency. Failing to embrace God's purposes for our life for the sake of the next generations is like throwing away unimaginable treasures into the sea.

# food for thought and discussion:

Read Nehemiah 1:1-11; 2:17-18

- Make a list of some of the significant changes in our culture that have occurred since you were a child. List the changes in one of the three categories below:

    **Positive**                    **Negative**                    **Uncertain**

- How did Nehemiah respond to the reports from Jerusalem?

- When was the last time you wept over the condition of your city? When was the last time you wept over your family or church?

- Whose sins did Nehemiah confess? Why?

- What would be an appropriate response to the cultural condition in our world? Consider these scriptures in your response: 2 Chron. 7:14; Judges 2:6-15; 2 Cor. 7:10

# action step:

Assume a posture of prayer and confess the sins of your generation and those who've gone before. Ask God to give you a genuinely repentant and receptive heart for what He wants to do through you. If you can, gather other grandparents together to do this with you. Check out our resources at *www. christiangrandparenting.net* under PRAYER to help you in this process.

# don't be a maybe boomer

g r a n d p a u s e :
*"Growing old is mandatory; growing up is optional."*
Chili Davis, former Major League Baseball player from Jamaica

**G**reg is a leading-edge Boomer, a guy at the upper end of his generation's age range. Rising at 5:30 each morning, he heads for an intense forty-five minute workout at the gym. After his workout, Greg makes a dinner reservation on his iPhone and sends a text to his wife to let her know he will pick her up at six. After responding to a text from his granddaughter, he checks in with his secretary, scrolls through his Facebook and Twitter posts, and downloads the latest *Wall Street Journal*. Before heading for the office, Greg stops at Starbucks for a mocha coconut frappuccino.

Greg's active, tech-filled lifestyle is typical of many Boomers. They often live life at full tilt, trying to ignore an emerging reality—growing old. Not all leading-edge baby boomers live like Greg. It is not, however, an exaggerations to say that the majority are as active at sixty as they were at forty. Many still think of themselves as relatively young.

According to one Associated Press article[1], most leading-edge baby boomers prefer to think of themselves as middle-aged. Though most feel very positive about being grandparents, Boomers still resist thinking of themselves as old.

Perhaps you've noticed the number of boomer-generation celebrities who work hard to maintain their once-youthful image. It is at times almost embarrassing, if not amusing. Yet it does reveal something about how Boomers see themselves. Rock stars like Bob Dylan, Mick Jagger, or members of The Who, stage their comeback appearances in an attempt to re-create an image they had thirty years earlier.

An earlier TV commercial lampooned this celebrity charade. It opens at a loud rock concert. The cameras zoom in on an energetic rock band on stage just as they're finishing their last song. The crowd goes crazy as the band heads for the dressing room. In the dressing room, the cameras expose what is really under all the make-up, wigs, and latex facial enhancements. A group of wrinkled seventy- and eighty-year-olds emerge from the cosmetic ruse.

We follow them as they leave their dressing room and shuffle their way down a long hallway and toward the waiting crowd outside. As they emerge, the screaming fans suddenly grow quiet as this group of elderly adults exits from backstage. The band members smile and go their way. Not making the connection, the crowd returns its attention to the stage door and resumes its chant for the band they had seen on stage moments before.

Celebrities aren't the only ones who go to great lengths to stay young looking. While I applaud the efforts of aging Boomers to stay active, the problem comes when we obsess about looking youthful. That's foolishness. Why? Because it is rooted in a lie that equates youth and outward attractiveness with a happy, purpose-filled life.

## shaking the tree

While many Boomers bristle at the *senior* label and take great pains to maintain a youthful image, the reality is that aging happens. We may try to delay its effects, but we cannot escape it. Becoming a grandparent has a way of shaking the tree of life and dropping a few nuts of reality in our path.

There is no lack of cultural markers to shake that tree for us as well. Diane and I had hardly settled into the fresh air as empty-nesters (if there is such a thing), when that dratted AARP invitation arrived in the mail with *my* name on it. Had it come to this already? To make matters worse, the stranger staring back at me in the mirror did little to reinforce my fictitious mental image of myself. The effects of gravity were in plain sight. There was no escaping it. The leading-edge baby boomers had come of age, and I was one of them.

The Teacher of Ecclesiastes made the observation that "generations come and generations go." He also said "there is a time to be born and a time to die." (I think he forgot to mention a time to grow old.) Whether we want to admit it or not, our only meaningful choice is to decide how we will deal with this unavoidable diminished thing called "aging" when, as the Teacher observes, *"strong men stoop, the grinders cease because they are few, and those looking through the window grow dim"* (Ecclesiastes. 12:3). Now that sounds like something to look forward to! So, while we can't stop it, we can choose how to deal with it.

I've decided to accept the inevitable, make the best of it, and seize the unimaginable opportunities that are still out there while I can. I'm in my mid-sixties as I write this, but I have to say that I don't feel old—most of the time.

It was baseball pitching great Satchel Paige who asked, "How old would you be if you didn't know how old you are?" Attitude has a lot to do with everything in life. Those who are paranoid about aging are often also obsessed with futile attempts to color it, tuck it, botox it, or otherwise cover it and pretend it away. Good luck with that!

The relentless effects of this diminished thing called aging come into proper perspective when we learn to embrace the delight of being God's workmanship at whatever stage of life we find ourselves. That is exactly what happens to most of us when that first grandchild arrives.

At that moment when your new grandson or granddaughter rests in your arms and you experience that overwhelming sense of joy, the things of life that really matter seem much clearer. With the exception of the birth of your first child (wasn't that just yesterday?), nothing compares to it. It's especially meaningful if you are privileged to be present when that moment arrives. In the ecstasy of that occasion, life is good, if only for a brief moment.

When that third-generation moment arrives, something else occurs as well. You discover that being a grandparent is beyond compare, and suddenly you don't really feel so old after all. At the very moment you are reminded how old you are, a euphoric infusion of youthful energy explodes into your being and you feel young again! It's like life has started all over. But here's the question that must be answered: Will you seize the moment and courageously engage God's purpose for you as a grandparent, or will you seek the easy way out?

The verdict is still out on how the baby boomers will do as grandparents. Our record as a generation of parents has not been so stellar. Will this emerging generation of grandparents step to the plate and hit the ball out of the park, or will we become nothing more than *maybe boomers* who never get on base?

Those of us in this demographic milieu stand among the swelling ranks of nearly two million new grandparents each year in America.2 It is estimated that by the year 2015 there will be more than one hundred million grandparents (that's 100,000,000!) in the United States—60 percent baby boomers.3 In fact, at the time of this writing, grandparents compose nearly twenty five percent of the total U.S. population.4 That's a lot of grandparents!

Boomer grandparents have the great distinction of being part of the youngest generation of grandparents in western civilization. The average age of *all* grandparents in this country at the time of this writing is around forty-eight.[5] Today's emerging grandparents are active, intellectually curious, and savvy about and wired into the latest technologies.

More than 60 percent of us are still in the workforce either full time or part time. Many of us have discretionary income and are generous with our money, especially when it comes to our grandchildren, spending more than fifty two billion dollars every year on our grandchildren alone.[6]

We love our grandchildren, want to spend time with them, and are often involved in significant caregiving roles with them. A startling statistic reveals that nearly seventy-two percent of today's grandparents take care of their grandchildren on a regular basis either as primary caregivers or occasional caregivers.[7] Even though we love all the benefits of being a grandparent, most of us were not prepared for all the additional responsibilities that have fallen upon us—responsibilities that now disrupt our original retirement plans and goals.

# when reality sinks in

Bob and Sharon (not their real names) are part of that exploding generation of boomer grandparents. Excited about the prospect of being grandparents, they were about to experience another kind of explosion that would turn their world upside down. The day their granddaughter, Paige, was born was a mixture of indescribable joy that only a grandparent can appreciate, and a somber realization that the plans they had made for the second half of their lives were about to vaporize.

The mental and emotional state of their daughter, Brenda, would likely make it difficult for her to function as a responsible mother. Adopted when she was less than a year old, their attempts as parents to communicate their deep love and affection for her received little response. Only much later did they learn about detachment disorder and its profound effect on so many adopted children, even in the most loving home environment.

Still, as devoted Christian parents, they did what they could to teach Brenda from God's Word and share the Lord's love and grace. They were thrilled when she prayed with them to receive Christ when she was eight. As a teenager she had been active in their church youth group and went on two youth missions trips. She appeared to be a normal teenager whose faith was strong and growing.

Then she met Trey in her senior year of high school. Things changed very quickly. Bob and Sharon's attempts to talk with her about Trey were met with either cold indifference or sudden outbursts of anger. The day she graduated from high school Brenda left home and moved in with Trey. Her life turned into one of sex, drugs, alcohol, and frequent bouts with the law. Within six months Brenda was pregnant. When Brenda refused to get an abortion her parents were grateful, After that, Trey quickly disappeared from her life.

Bob and Sharon were encouraged when Brenda decided to move back home. They hoped this would be the start of some positive new beginnings. Unfortunately, Brenda never severed the connections with her 'friends' in the drug scene. Seven months later, she was in jail for aggravated robbery and drug possession. She was sentenced to six years in prison.

After a very long and expensive legal process, Bob and Sharon were able to get full custody of their granddaughter and eventually full legal adoption rights. Now, not only were they grandparents, but parents once again in their early fifties. They found themselves among the nearly three million, and growing, grandparents nationwide serving as primary caregivers to their grandchildren.

While Bob and Sharon's story represents a relatively small percentage of all grandparents, their story is becoming increasingly more common. Many Boomers are reaping what they sowed in their younger years as parents. Many others are forced to deal with difficult situations not of their making. Whatever the cause or circumstances, filling the grandparent role suddenly becomes something very different than these grandparents could have ever imagined possible.

Most Boomers really do love being grandparents and find it the single most satisfying thing in life. That's good news. Most of us also believe we can do a better job with our grandchildren than we did with our own children. Maybe… that still remains to be seen.

## start your engines

I'm not really a NASCAR fan, but I did enjoy watching the final laps of the 2011 Daytona 500 NASCAR race in which Trevor Bayne. At twenty years of age he became the youngest driver to ever win this prestigious race. It was quite a feat in a sport dominated by the *old boys* of racing.

Boomers, and now leading-edge Gen Xers', are the youngest and most active grandparents in this country's history. Like Trevor Bayne, we are making our mark in a 'race' that was previously an *old boys* club. We may look younger and be more active than our parents or grandparents, but how will we fare in this new role?

We must be willing to set aside our own script and follow God's script for this new chapter of the story He is writing for us and for the next generations. It is a story filled with surprises and challenges, but it is a rewarding journey. The enormous challenges will require steadfast courage and unyielding commitment. In the end, if we put our trust in God and persevere, we will be rewarded. Most importantly, our grandchildren will be blessed.

Will we come to the starting line ready to race, sold out and intentional about making history by finishing well? Or will we go down in history as the 'Maybe Boomers', more preoccupied with doing our own thing, protecting our own portfolios, and pursuing personal comfort than being a conduit of blessing for the next generations?

We're about to find out. Boomer grandparents…start your engines!

# food for thought and discussion:

- How do you think today's Boomer (and GenX) grandparents are doing as intentional grandparents today? Why?

- Do you agree that many Boomer grandparents are not prepared for the responsibilities we will be facing? Why or why not?

- What are the challenges you are facing as a new or experienced grandparent today? Do you feel you have all the resources and support you need to fulfill your role successfully? Why or why not?

- What do you believe our most important role should be as a grandparent? Why?

# action step:

Ask your grandchildren and adult children to tell you what things in your life they think most represent what is important to you. Do these measure up with the legacy you want to leave?

# allies or adversaries?

*Children's children are a crown to the aged, and parents are the pride of their children.*
Proverbs 17:6

Chelsea dreaded going to her mother-in-law's home for the holidays. In spite of an otherwise good relationship, she knew the tension would be thick. The tension was due to her mother-in-law's consistent violation of rules Chelsea and her husband, Dan, wanted enforced. Mostly it was about what the kids were allowed to eat and their allowable bed time—oh, and some occasional unsolicited advice concerning childrearing.

If Chelsea tried to say something about the rule violations, her mother-in-law reprimanded her for depriving the children of the fun things grandkids should enjoy with their grandparents. Chelsea knew the kids would eat any junk food Grandma put out. They would also be allowed to stay up late to watch TV or a movie if she or Dan did not put a stop to it. Chelsea also resented the collateral damage they would be left to clean up when they returned home. Why couldn't Dan's mother simply respect their rules and boundaries for the kids? Why was it so hard to work together?

Sound familiar? Okay, I know you don't see the grandkids that often so the rules should flex a little when they are at your house, right? After all, that's why the grandkids love coming to your house. They look forward to doing things at Grandma and Grandpa's they can't do at home. Do I sense some devilish delight in the old saw that says grandparents and grandkids get along so well because they have a common enemy? Pay back time!

If you buy into that way of thinking you probably also buy into the notion that grandparenting is primarily about the grandparents and the grandkids doing *their* thing together. As tempting as it may be to take that approach to grandparenting, I hope I can convince you otherwise.

Successful grandparents know it is not just about the grandkids and them. I hope you recognize that our top priority is to figure out how parents and grandparents can work together as allies, not adversaries. Our goal is to work together towards the same objective—to help our grandchildren become all God wants them to be. Our job is to find ways to foster an environment in which our adult children can become the greatest parents possible. It's what courageous grandparents do. The moment we start to think and act independently or judgmentally, there will be trouble right here in River City.

There was a time when this God-designed alliance between parent and grandparent was more typical in family life, though not without its share of challenges. Still, those were much less complicated times for families. Children generally had only one set of parents and two sets of grandparents. If the grandparents were still living, they often lived in the same community— maybe even next door. My wife and I both grew up in that kind of community environment. That is not the typical scenario in America today.

## getting it together

Roughly half of today's children have multiple sets of parents and grandparents, often separated by great distances. Divorce has dramatically changed the landscape of family dynamics. Grandparents must now cope with a myriad of complicating factors created by divorce and remarriage. Because the family tribe rarely lives together anymore, families often exist independently in their own cultural groups with differing values and traditions. This has exponentially complicated the ability to navigate this cultural mix of blended families and find a way to maintain family cohesion.

In spite of these obstacles, the importance of a mutually supportive partnership remains unchanged. It may be more complicated, but it is still important and achievable in most cases. In fact, the need for such a partnership is made even more necessary by these complications.

It will always be true that a mutually cooperative partnership between parent and grandparent is one of the most satisfying and productive relationships on the planet. On the other hand, an uncooperative relationship with adult children and their spouses will likely unleash a tsunami of debris and destruction among family members in which few winners emerge.

Everyone knows, including the children, that the kids pay the heaviest price in incompatible family relationships. Conflict between parents, not to mention parents and grandparents, leave the children caught in the middle as mediators. That is not where children belong.

In Dan and Chelsea's situation, they knew something had to be done or things would only get worse…for everyone. They wanted something better for themselves, Dan's mom, and their children. In the long run, they knew everyone would lose if something didn't change. So, they chose to sit down together with Dan's mom to talk about the situation.

They were surprised to learn that Dan's mother truly believed it was necessary for her to give the grandkids junk food and to let them stay up late. Why? Because if she didn't, she was convinced they would not like her or want to visit.

"It's what grandparents do," she explained. "They know they can do things at Grandma's they can't do at home. Why deprive them of that? Besides, it's only once a year."

That revelation opened up an opportunity for Dan and Chelsea to share a different point of view.

"Mom, we appreciate your wanting to give the kids a good time," they explained. "We want them to like you, too, but you're wrong in assuming that having a 'good time' or how much they like you are based upon the quantity of junk food you stuff in them or how late they are allowed to stay up. If what they eat and what time they go to bed is all there is to measure your worth as their grandmother then something is wrong. These are not the things that determine how good a grandparent you are. They have nothing to do with whether they like you or don't like you. When you ignore and violate our rules we have set up for their benefit, you make us out to be the 'bad guys'. We promise you they will still like you even if you follow our rules."

I'm convinced that if more parents displayed the same kind of courage and profound wisdom expressed by Dan and Chelsea, a lot of family heartache could be averted. Their willingness to openly talk about the problem cleared the air and made it possible to lay a foundation for a mutually satisfying partnership that was a win-win for everyone, especially the kids.

So many conflicts could be resolved if the effort was made to talk about them with humility and honesty. It took a lot of courage for Dan and Chelsea to initiate that conversation and get the real issue on the table. They did it because their relationship with Grandma, and her relationship with the grandkids, was too important to ignore. I am convinced most parents want their kids to have a positive relationship with their grandparents just as much as the grandparents do. For that to happen, somebody needs to step to the plate and put the ball in play.

The conversation with Dan's mom ought to give all of us something to think about. Will it really make that much difference in your relationship with your grandkids if you enforce some of the boundaries their parents feel are important while at your house? Obviously, some are convinced it will make a difference. I hope Dan and Chelsea can change your thinking. If these things are the only meaningful connections we have with our grandchildren, something is indeed terribly wrong. Either our understanding of what constitutes an effective grandparent is deficient, or we are pathological. It might be worth doing some self-examination and then consider a different viewpoint.

## bite your lip

Without question, the majority of comments and requests for help that I receive from grandparents involve their relationships with their adult children. Their questions generally fall into two categories:

- How do I deal with hostility by one or both parents towards any overt discussion about my Christian faith?

- How do I cope with the resentment I feel relative to matters of power and control when I'm around the grandkids, particularly in areas of discipline, rules, and parental boundaries?

Should you be one of those grandparents blessed with a positive relationship with your adult children and their spouses, guard that relationship and keep it strong. For the rest, remember that many of the tensions experienced in our relationships with our adult children emanate from differing philosophies of childrearing.

There are times when I look at the way my own adult children parent and often wonder where they learned those things. There seems to be very little resemblance to the way my wife and I parented. That may not be all bad, I suppose, but the temptation is to step in and 'offer some sound advice.'

There may be times when giving advice or taking even more drastic measures is appropriate, and even necessary. This is especially true in the case of a potentially harmful situation. I can think of at least three areas in which such intervention may be necessary: 1) unethical actions; 2) immoral behavior; or 3) unsafe situations that have the potential for serious personal harm.

For example, it's one thing to say something if a small child is left alone without supervision in the bathtub; the safety of the child is at issue. It's quite another matter when that same small child splashes around in the dog's water dish while Mom's at home. It isn't a moral or safety issue then; it's a parental matter.

When it comes to personal preferences about parenting, housekeeping, or other personal life choices, however, more often than not, our advice might better be kept to ourselves. Remember, our grandchildren could be the ones most negatively affected by any interference or potential rift that might develop. This is where wisdom is needed. Our goal is the parents' success in raising their child. We need to know when it's appropriate to speak and when it's time to keep our opinions to ourselves. Here's some advice about giving advice: *Don't offer any unless asked*.

There is no shortage of heartbreaking circumstances leading to conflict in parent-child relationships. Most grandparents, however, know that few things are more devastating than being torn from a relationship with a grandchild or grandchildren resulting from conflict with a parent. It's impossible to describe the pain of being denied the opportunity to see or communicate with a grandchild. How does one bear the gut-wrenching agony that rips at the heart of grandparents who are forbidden to speak of their faith in any form around their own grandchildren? How do we find solace in the midst of the mountains of guilt that surround us, knowing that we neglected our own responsibility as a parent? Suddenly that neglect appears to threaten all hope of a positive relationship with an adult child, and consequently, our grandchildren. So what do we do?

There is no quick fix for any of these painful scenarios, but there is hope. The journey will certainly be a difficult and sometimes painful one. While the outcome cannot be guaranteed, in most cases, something good and positive can and will rise from the ashes of these crumbled relationships.

If you are a grandparent embroiled in difficult relationships with your adult children, I want you to know that you are not alone. Let me say it again—*you are not alone*. At times, all that is needed is for someone to help you step back from the forest so you can see the trees and get some perspective. My prayer is that God will grant you that perspective and that you will trust Him by clinging to the lifeline of hope and grabbing on to the handholds of grace. Only then can you begin the upward climb towards a positive and productive relationship with your adult children and their spouses.

Never lose sight of the fact that the circumstances of a difficult relationship may be beyond your control. In fact, it may have *nothing* whatsoever to do with you or anything you may have done. But it does not mean *nothing* can be done. I plead with you not to lose heart or give up seeking resolution and reconciliation.

## perception is everything

Perception is everything in relationships. Whether or not we are to blame for something gone awry in a relationship is not the issue unless we are too proud to admit we are to blame. What is important is to understand how others perceive us so we can seek God's wisdom and grace to correct any wrong perceptions. Only then can trust be rebuilt. Until we are able to correct those things that may justify negative perceptions, the strain in the relationship will continue.

When my daughter went through a divorce a number of years ago, I was angry and devastated. I could not understand what was going on. From my point of view, my reaction towards her was reasonable. From her perspective, my attitude and responses were condemning and unreasonable.

I stubbornly clung to my pride for a long time. I convinced myself that, even though I disapproved of her decision (and, of course, I must be right), she knew I still loved her. Thankfully my wife finally stepped in and reminded me that *my* point of view was not the issue. The issue was my daughter's perception that my love for her was conditional. She also reminded me that if our daughter continued to pull away, it could mean our grandson might be pulled away as well. Is that what I wanted? I hate it when she's right.

After some wallowing in self-pity, I was finally able to swallow my pride and speak to my daughter. I confessed that I had not done a good job of showing her unconditional love when we disagreed. Even though I might never agree about the decision she made, I could never stop loving her and wanting God's best for her. That was a huge turning point for both of us. By the grace of God, a relationship I had almost given up on was restored. Of equal importance was the preservation of my cherished bond with my grandson, who remains the joy of my life.

While every family situation is different, the whole point of this chapter is fixed. I've said it several times. Let me say it again. Effective grandparenting is a more achievable goal if you can maintain, as much as is in your power to do so, a strong, healthy relationship with your grandchildren's parents. That's what courageous grandparents do.  Shall I say it again?

This divine alliance is a key component for keeping the conduit of God's blessing unclogged. There is always something *you* can do to positively impact your relationship with your adult children. The wall of personal conflict can sometimes seem insurmountable, but with God nothing is impossible.

In His all-sufficient grace He has provided us with four essential *handholds* for climbing over that seemingly impossible wall of conflict toward positive relationships with our adult children—or anyone for that matter. Each handhold focuses on a specific aspect of godly character that impacts our relationships. As we climb and grip the handholds provided, what was impossible becomes possible. So grab your climbing gear—let's do some climbing together!

# food for thought and discussion:

- How would you describe the relationship you have with your adult children and their spouses right now? Can you identify in any way with the challenges Dan and Chelsea faced with their children's grandmother? How?

- Do you agree that perception is everything? Why or why not? How important is perception in being able to remove obstacles in that relationship?

- What is the difference between enjoying your grandchildren and spoiling them?

- How important are the relationships we have with our adult children? What are you willing to do to preserve and protect those relationships?

# action steps:

Sit down with your adult children, tell them you want to do everything you can to help them succeed as the greatest parents possible for your grandchildren, and ask them to respond to these questions:

- What things do we do that make it difficult for you to be the parents you want to be?

- How can we better partner with you to help you be successful parents and raise children that will have the chance to be all they are capable of being?

# get a grip!

### g r a n d p a u s e :

*"A person's character is accurately measured by his reaction to life's inequities."*

Unknown

**M**y niece is an avid rock climber. She knows the importance of a good handhold whether scaling the side of a vertical cliff or an indoor climbing wall. A good hold versus a poor hold is the difference between success and failure in a climb—which means something very different on an indoor climbing wall than it does on the side of a mountain cliff.

A good hold, however, is only as good as an individual's grip. She also knows there are at least four other key elements required for a safe, successful climb: 1) Using your feet like your hands. You can stand on your feet a lot longer than you can hang by your arms; 2) Using the right equipment—no short cuts here; 3) Having a trustworthy belayer (the person at the bottom who holds the rope and is your lifeline should you fall). If you worry about the belayer, you can't focus on the climb; and 4) Conquering your fears; focus on where you're going, and look down only as far as your feet.

Good climbers have learned to put their confidence in their training, their equipment, their belayer, and the various holds and anchors in the rock. While fear is normal, they understand that if a climber cannot overcome fear, either he will be unable to continue the climb, or he will lose his grip and fall.

Like climbing, scaling the cliffs of life can be dangerous. Sometimes family relationships can feel like standing at the foot of an unassailable mountain. Yet, with the right equipment and God as our *belayer*, we are free to stay focused on the climb. Trust the various 'holds' God has put in place for scaling the steep walls of life. He promised that, *"His divine power has given us everything we need for life and godliness through our knowledge of Him who called us by His own glory and goodness"* (2 Peter 1:3). Believe it with all your heart. This is the source of our confidence to reach up, grab hold… and climb.

The following four handholds offer hope to scale the wall of conflict and maintain a strong partnership with your adult children and their spouses. They are found in Ephesians 4:2-3: *"Be completely humble and gentle; be patient, bearing with one another in love. Make every effort to keep the unity of the Spirit through the bond of peace."* These are secure holds for navigating every relationship of life. Let's explore them together.

# handhold #1 – humility
*"Be completely **humble** and gentle…"*

Rick and Judy both use the word *sensitive* to describe his mother's relationship with their children. It's a word that has to do, not only with the way she imparts her spiritual heritage to them, but the unconditional love she always expresses towards her grandkids. "Even when they don't make the decisions that she might, she loves them unconditionally. Her greatest gift to her grandchildren is to cover them with prayer every day," Rick observed. "Because of her humble, sensitive spirit, her grandchildren and great-grandchildren know they are loved unconditionally. I don't think there's anything either of us would change about how my mother plays out her role as a grandmother."

Pride and humility cannot co-exist. One is nurtured by the grand illusion of self-sufficiency and self-importance—a crumbling handhold that will lead to a fall. The other is cultivated in the selfless notion of losing oneself—foolishness in the world's eyes, but the surest handhold for a successful climb.

Humility insists on the interests of others over our own, and actually leads us to see them as better than ourselves, according to Philippians 2:3. Sounds rather radical, doesn't it? Does that mean we should consider our children's parenting skills, or our perceived lack of them, as better than all our years of experience as a parent? Maybe—maybe not. But is it so unimaginable to consider that God has just as adequately equipped them as He did us to be successful parents to our grandchildren? Even if they aren't doing a great job, can we look through the clutter and give them our support?

Humility acknowledges our humanness with all its limitations. It allows us to rise above our humanity and rest in Him who knows better than we ever will.

Acknowledging our own limitations frees us to own up to our mistakes, including those we made as parents. Humility sets us free to admit that we may not have all the answers, nor do we always see things as clearly as we might like to think. It liberates us in the security of God's grace to lay down our mantel of authority long enough to empty ourselves and extend the hand of a servant.

Courageous grandparents are humble grandparents respecting and honoring the boundaries of our adult children even when it isn't comfortable (assuming there is no imminent danger or serious injury involved). It is foolish to bypass the humility handhold by insisting on doing things our way and expect to reach the summit of possibilities God has in mind for our family relationships—to the praise of His glory and the blessing of all.

Here's something all of us would do well to remember: *"He guides the humble in what is right and teaches them His way"* (Ps. 25:9).

# handhold #2 – patience

*"Be completely humble and gentle; **be patient**..."*

A farmer who grows and harvests the Chinese bamboo tree understands patience. He knows that his reward for watering and fertilizing efforts during the first year will yield nothing more than a tiny sprout barely an inch high. Throughout the second year there are no signs of growth whatsoever. The seasons come and go for another three years, and still the farmer has nothing to show for all of his hours of labor getting this stubborn tree to grow.

In the fifth year, however, the farmer's patience pays off. Just when he might be tempted to lay down the watering can and give up, a sprout suddenly appears and grows at an astonishing rate. Before the end of that year's growing season, the tree that showed no signs of life for five years will soar up to ninety feet—that's nine stories in less than a year!

Now, I am not a particularly patient person. Just ask my family. I like to see results—right now! I need constant reminders that truly important things in life often require enormous amounts of patience. Unfortunately you and I live in a quick-fix world and have been trained to expect what we want when we want it. Whether losing weight, recovering from an injury or illness, getting service at a restaurant, or getting through rush hour traffic, we want it fast. When the driver in front of me isn't moving when the light changes, impatience makes me want to scream, *The light won't get any greener, lady!* When it comes to dealing with fractured relationships, it is tempting to be equally impatient.

Proverbs 15:18 says, *"A hot-tempered man stirs up dissension, but a patient man calms a quarrel."* Ouch! If patience can be such a powerful healing agent, why do I so impatiently react when things don't progress the way I want? Perhaps Paul provides a clue in Colossians 3 when he explains that patience is the offspring of holiness and forgiveness clothed in kindness, gentleness, compassion, and humility. Patience exalts the worth of another rather than my agenda. It rests confidently in the providential work of God in others...and in me, in God's time.

Patience sprouts in the soil of faith where the roots of unshakable belief in God and His Word grow deep. It is confident in the knowledge that the work God is doing in me, and in my family, is good enough. I am an instrument of God's grace, but I don't make the seeds grow. Since I can't control the outcome, it would be foolish to attempt to *fix* things. That usually means I end up creating a royal mess, especially in my own family.

How long did it take for the Chinese bamboo to grow to ninety feet? Six months, a year? No, it was *five years*! In that five-year period every drop of water, every ounce of fertilizer, and every hour of care the farmer provided made a difference. Deep in the soil, obscured from sight, a large network of roots had been growing so the tree would have a firm foundation. If the farmer were to get impatient and worry that it may die, any attempt to make it grow faster could have stopped its growth and undermined the root system necessary for it to grow and remain strong.

Flourishing growth is the fruit of patience and perseverance. It applies not only to growing a Chinese bamboo tree, but to people. As grandparents it's easy for us to want to jump in there and fix things. Be patient… and watch God do an amazing thing when the time is right.

# handhold #3 – forgiveness
*"Be completely humble and gentle; be patient,*
***bearing with one another in love…"***

Forgiveness was the big issue that built a wall between my daughter and me after her divorce. It had become a personal issue for me. I harbored a great deal of anger towards her throughout the ordeal because of all the injury to our family, and especially my grandson. If I were honest, I would have to acknowledge that I was more focused on my hurt and embarrassment than I was willing to admit. Even though I loved her, my unforgiving heart placed a barrier between us.

Deep hurt carried around in an unforgiving heart is like large stones constantly being stacked one on another until a massive rock wall is erected across the path of reconciliation. Soon a root of bitterness sprouts and begins to spread like a vine across the wall of the heart like an aggressive cancer. Allowed to grow it can be very difficult to cut out, destroying relationships and blocking the way to reconciliation. Forgiveness cuts out the roots of bitterness and slices through the web of malice entangling a wounded heart. It stirs a lifeless heart to life like tulips in spring. It tears down the wall of bitterness so that peace and unity can flourish.

It's easy to talk about forgiveness when we want to be forgiven. It's quite another matter when we are called upon to forgive another who has deeply injured us—the kind of injury that occurs when a son-in-law or daughter-in-law refuses to let us see our grandchildren. Paul exhorts us to *"get rid of all bitterness, rage and anger, brawling and slander, along with every form of malice. Be kind and compassionate to one another, forgiving each other, just as in Christ God forgave you"* (Ephesians 4:31-32).

Forgiveness springs to life when two things happen: 1) we realize how much we have been forgiven; and 2) we acknowledge how much we need to be forgiven—the Bible calls that repentance. Understanding how much I have been forgiven frees me to forgive others. Repentance also opens the door for those whom I have wronged to forgive me.

The best grip on this handhold happens when we identify the stuff in those relationships with our adult children and their spouses, kneel before the Father who has forgiven us in Christ, and ask God take away the bitterness and anger. Say out loud, "I forgive _____ for the hurt I have received. I will believe the best, not the worst."

Then we need to ask God to show us where we have injured a son, daughter or in-law, and seek his or her forgiveness. We must avoid making excuses or justifying ourselves. We admit where we have injured other in their eyes, and ask for forgiveness.

Forgiveness, like cholesterol-fighting medication for the heart, unclogs the arteries so that God's lavish and extravagant grace can freely flow through us and bring healing for everyone involved. Because we are forgiven, we are free to forgive, to love, and to bless. So, while an unforgiving heart will shut the door to healthy relationships, forgiveness opens it and keeps it open. I suspect you know what I'm talking about.

# handhold #4 – blessing

*"Be completely humble and gentle; be patient, bearing with one another in love.*
***Make every effort to keep the unity of the Spirit in the bond of peace."***

Howie was born into a broken home. He was left with his paternal grandmother who raised him. In elementary school, Howie was quite adept at causing trouble. His teachers passed him to the next grade, even when his grades weren't good enough, because they did not want him in their class again. His fifth grade teacher predicted that five boys in his class would end up in prison. He was told he would be one of the five. The teacher was right about three of them. That teacher, Miss Simon, once tied him to his seat with a rope and taped his mouth shut.

Then he met his sixth grade teacher, Miss Noe. She told him something that would change his life forever. "I've heard a lot about you, Howie," she said, "but I don't believe a word of it." She began to speak words of hope and blessing into his life that had never been spoken to him before. She broke the curse of negativity and showed him that she cared enough to say, 'Howie, I believe in you!' From that life-changing moment, Howie discovered the truth about God's purpose for his life and the high value he possessed as a person created in the image of God.

As an adult Howie went on to become a well-known author, speaker, and professor of Christian education at Dallas Seminary until his death in February 2013. The impact of his life on others would be impossible to measure. His name is Dr. Howard G. Hendricks, one of the most respected evangelical speakers and authors in the twentieth century.* In the words of the late Paul Harvey, "Now, you know the rest of the story"!

The blessing handhold is a key hold in life that grips a heart and promotes peace and unity in family relationships. We'll deal with this more in chapter 14.

For now, I want you to grasp the fact that the peace Paul speaks of here is proactive. Words are powerful weapons for peace and unity. Gossip, complaining, and cursing produce dissension. Words of blessing—intentionally speaking well of another—promote unity and peace. That especially true in our families.

Speaking blessing into someone's life never goes out of style or loses its power. That's why Paul wrote, *"Do not let any unwholesome talk come out of your mouths, but only what is helpful for building others up according to their needs, that it may benefit those who listen"* (Ephesians 4:29). I think Howie could vouch for that.

God isn't interested in excuses on this matter. His command is straight forward concerning the 'wholesome talk' issue. In another of Paul's letters, he makes it clear that building up others involves getting rid of *"all anger, rage, malice, slander and filthy language from your lips"* and clothing ourselves with *"compassion, kindness, humility, gentleness and patience"* (Colossians 3:8, 12).

The words we speak have the power to bless or curse. Instead of expressing our opinion, why not put an arm around our adult children, look them in the eye, and speak genuine words of blessing? Tell them how valued and loved they are. Remind them how cherished they are to God, how He desires to pour out His favor upon them, longs to prosper them as parents. We have the power to speak blessing or cursing. It is the handhold of blessing that will get us over the wall.

## clip In and climb

Don't expect this climb to be easy. Just because we do our part doesn't mean all the bad stuff will automatically turn into really good stuff. We cannot control how our adult children will respond. They have to make their own choices. We can only pray they will choose to join the climb on the other side of the wall.

There are things we do have control over—things that can trigger a parent's withdrawal or hostility. That's what this climb is all about. We decide whether the relationship will be molded by humility, forgiveness, patience, and blessing, or whether it will be characterized by arrogance, condemnation, impatience, and cursing. It's our choice. One set of handholds will hold in even the most trying conditions. The other set will crumble in our grip. It is important to get a grip on the right holds.

The apostle Paul challenged the strong believer in Romans 14:13 with this instruction: *"Stop passing judgment on one another. Instead, make up your mind not to put any stumbling block or obstacle in your brother's way."* Could that also mean a son and daughter-in-law? Hold on, there's more: *"Let us therefore make every effort to do what leads to peace and to mutual edification"* (vs 19).

Sounds like some pretty wise counsel for those of us who care about the relationships we have with our families. Making every effort means not giving up. It means we keep on climbing even when our muscles are aching and it seems the progress is slow. Take a cue from the Chinese bamboo tree, and trust that God is doing a good work through us and in spite of us. It's worth the wait to see the relationship with our adult children suddenly spring to life. It's worth the effort to hope for that joyous moment when we can hold our precious grandchildren close.

Whether the relationship we have with our adult children is horrible, wonderful, or somewhere in between, the rope has been tossed to us. It is up to us to clip in and scale the walls that hinder those relationships with the handholds God has provided. There is too much at stake if we don't try. Remember, we have everything we need for a successful climb. The handholds are strong. Our belayer, the heavenly Father, will never let go. There is no need to fear. So…grab the rope, reach up, and climb!

## food for thought and discussion:

- Which of the handholds discussed in this chapter are most difficult for you to grip? Why?

- What other handholds do you think might also be considered?

## action step:

If you are in a group, pray for each other in the area of your greatest struggle with these handholds. If you are not in a group, find another godly person who will help you and pray for you in these areas. Then set up a plan for implementing these four handholds intentionally in your relationship with your adult children.

## p a r t    t w o

# WISE UP!

*Sanballat was very angry when he learned that we were rebuilding the wall. He flew into a rage and mocked the Jews, saying in front of his friends and the Samarian army officers, "What does this bunch of poor, feeble Jews think they are doing? Do they think they can build the wall in a day if they offer enough sacrifices? Look at those charred stones they are pulling out of the rubbish and using again!"*

*Tobiah the Ammonite, who was standing beside him, remarked, "That stone wall would collapse if even a fox walked along the top of it!"*

*Then the people of Judah began to complain that the workers were becoming tired. There was so much rubble to be moved that we could never get it done by ourselves….*

*Then as I looked over the situation, I called together the leaders and the people and said to them, "Don't be afraid of the enemy! Remember the Lord, who is great and glorious, and fight for your friends, your families, and your homes!"*

*When our enemies heard that we knew of their plans and that God had frustrated them, we all returned to our work on the wall.*

Excerpted from Nehemiah, Chapters 4 and 6 (NLT)

*"Men of Issachar, who understood the times and knew what Israel should do…"*

1 Chronicles 12:32a (NIV)

# fly-shop wisdom

*…A people without understanding will come to ruin!*

Hosea 4:14

I've had the good fortune to fly-fish with my friend, Travis—an avid, skilled fly fisherman. I'm not a passionate fisherman like Travis, though I do enjoy the thrill of wading into a fast-moving mountain stream in the Rockies and soaking in the sights and sounds of God's magnificent handiwork.

One thing Travis taught me was that successful fly-fishing involves much more than being able to cast well. It is equally important to understand the environment and what the fish are feeding on in a particular location. A fisherman who doesn't know the nature of the fish he's trying to catch or their feeding habits won't catch many fish. That's why Travis always stopped by the local fly shop to talk with the resident guide about what the fish were biting at the time. He knew the wrong fly would result in a disappointing day.

I suspect King David knew little about fly-fishing, but like a good fisherman he did know a great deal about the importance of surrounding himself with people who understood the times. Scripture notes the peculiar quality among the men of the tribe of Issachar that set them apart from the other fighting men in David's service. These men were brave and skilled fighting men, but their particular asset was as *men who understood the times and knew what to do* (1 Chronicles 12:32). Among all the fighting men that had come to support David, the men of Issachar alone were singled out as men known for this unique wisdom and insight.

Why was this so significant? Because David was wise enough to understand that the outcome of the battles they would face required more than skill and bravery. As a leader he knew his own limits. He needed men who understood the enemy they would face—men who knew how to engage these foes with the resources they had.

These mighty men brought to David a spirit of discernment that kept things in perspective according to God's plans and purposes. It was a time of uncertainty. Wisdom and clear thinking were required. The men of Issachar had both.

Such wise, clear thinking is just as vital in our day as it was in David's. Our children and grandchildren need wise men and women in their lives with Issachar-like discernment. They deserve godly role models who see the world around them, *get it*, and have the courage do the right thing. Grandparents are poised to stand in the gap as the modern-day equivalent of the men of Issachar. The only question yet to be answered is whether today's grandparents will embrace this vital role wholeheartedly, or abdicate it in favor of a more comfortable retirement lifestyle.

Neglect and apathy as Christian parents and grandparents has allowed Satan to have his way far too long. In these chaotic and evil times this generation is being seduced by a pied piper's smooth-sounding tunes down a path that ends in destruction. It's time to wake up and wise up to what we are allowing to happen on our watch!

Consider this. At no other time in America are more grandparents living at one time as are living today. Imagine what could be accomplished if a committed throng of courageous, God-fearing grandparents went to their knees, sought God's wisdom, then rolled up their sleeves and linked arms to rebuild the crumbling walls of truth and faith in our land. How will this throng of grandparents respond?

If we embrace our responsibility to live wisely and courageously, I believe there are yet some amazing opportunities to be a conduit of God's transformational power for His kingdom. To make the most of those opportunities we need to make sure we have the right *fly* on the line before we cast out. There's too much at stake if we get it wrong.

So, let's stop by the 'fly shop' and see what we can learn about our grandchildren's world, a very different world from the one we knew as children.

## the postmodern delusion

It *is* the best of times and the most evil of times—to paraphrase a famous quote. Postmodernism and its birth mother, modernism, try to explain life apart from God. While modernism stressed the individual's freedom of expression and experimentation, it also rejected transcendent truth. It claimed that the world could be understood, not through revelation, but by reason.

Today's *postmodernism* is the logical extension of modernism. This worldview pushes individualism to the extreme rejecting the notion of a truth narrative for human existence. Absolute truth, for all practical purposes, is discarded in favor of individual choice which trumps everything, including God's moral law.

The supremacy of individualism means that truth is determined by an individual's feelings and level of comfort in coping with life. How that looks or feels can and does change almost daily. The societal cost of such thinking is enormous—community is devalued, tradition is debunked, ethics are ridiculed, and authority in scorned in favor of individual freedom. Self-restraint and self-sacrifice are rarely practiced.

Modernism and postmodernism perpetrate the fantasy that men can find happiness by their own ingenuity. At its core is the notion that God is irrelevant to any kind of human happiness and that individuals should be free to define who God is and what truth is according to what is useful to them or makes them happy. *"There is a way that seems right to man,"* Proverbs 16:25 declares, *"but in the*

*end it leads to death."* At the end of the day, the inane pursuit of happi︙
from God ends up impaled upon the sword of despair.

So what does any of this have to do with grandparenting? More than you
might think. How well do you understand the postmodern world? It is in times
like these that wise elders who understand the times are most needed. Job poses
the rhetorical question, *"Is not wisdom found among the aged? Does not long life
bring understanding?"* (Job 12:12).

The obvious answer is that it should, which is what Job argued. Unfortunately,
it is not always so. Wisdom is more than accumulated knowledge or life
experience. Without an understanding of who God is, who we are and why we are
here, foolishness substitutes for wisdom under the guise of 'enlightened thinking'.

The postmodern lie spins an alluring web of deception that snags its
unsuspecting victims in a curse of hopelessness. Lest you be tempted to doubt
the devastation of this deception, let me offer a few examples of how the lies of
a postmodern worldview are infecting and decomposing our world. If we are to
help our grandchildren counter the destruction produced by these lies, we need
to understand what they claim and the consequences.

## the modern family

Once-popular TV shows about the family such as *The Waltons*, *Leave It to
Beaver*, and *The Cosby Show*, gradually drifted toward shows like *All in the Family*,
*The Simpsons*, and *Modern Family*. These modern shows reflect a postmodern
redefinition of family. Marriage and family culture have shifted away from what
God established for our blessing and the good of mankind.

Many new television sitcoms, movies, and books satirize marriage as a
curse or restraint rather than a liberating, fulfilling relationship in which family
and society find an anchor against the storms of life. This rapid demise of the
traditional, historical understanding of both marriage and family is being fueled
by three prevailing cultural norms, which might more accurately be described as
'abnormalities'. I believe these cultural norms are actually curses with devastating
consequences that erode the essential foundations of a strong, stable society. The
time has come to for us to gear up, go fishing, and expose the lies for what they are.

## abnormality #1: divorce
### (Reconstructing Marriage and Family)

Divorce is the logical conclusion of marriages built on the shifting foundation
of a *what's-in-it-for-me* attitude. This view of marriage spread rapidly during the
*Enlightenment* period of the eighteenth century. Tim Keller, pastor and author of

*The Meaning of Marriage,* describes the Enlightenment as a time that "privatized marriage, taking it out of the public sphere. During this period the purpose of marriage was redefined to simply be for individual gratification, not any 'broader goal' such as reflecting God's nature, producing character, or raising children."[1]

While there are circumstances in which divorce is unavoidable, the truth is that the prevalence of no-fault divorce has redefined God's design for family today. The selfish interests of the husband and/or wife are regularly given more weight than the obvious wreckage caused to the rest of the family and our society.

Godly grandparents have a responsibility and opportunity to rectify this by example and by speaking the truth about the sanctity of marriage and family. Transparency, authenticity and integrity are needed to cultivate an environment of trust so the truth can be received. I highly recommend Tim Keller's book as a resource to help you in this task.

It's time to reclaim the truth about marriage—what it is and why it is so important. Grandparents are in a unique position to show the world the true glory and greatness of God's design for marriage—how a good marriage works. We have an opportunity to shape a view of marriage among our grandchildren that is healthy, enduring and a blessing to all.

## abnormality #2: cohabitation
### (Redefining Family)

Recent research suggests that the divorce rate in the United States is back to what it was in the early 1960s. Unfortunately, it is not all good news. The fact is that fewer couples are bothering to tie the knot, opting instead to live together.

According to a study conducted by the Center for Marriage and Family at the Institute for American Values, and the National Marriage Projects at the University of Virginia, cohabitation has skyrocketed since 1970.[2] The study reports that nearly fifty percent of all children live in a home where the adults live together but are not married. Many grandparents know too well the challenges these situations produce in their own families.

Even researchers admit that every child needs a 'forever family'. They confirm that children benefit significantly when their biological mother and father are living in a committed marriage. Why is this message not proclaimed in the public square?

Grandparents have a responsibility to battle on the front lines for marriage and family as God designed it. We cannot allow the enemy to steal this gift God instituted for the common good of spouses, children, extended family, and society as a whole. We need to talk about what marriage really is and model in our homes.

Today's grandparents must be intentional about partnering with their adult children to help them be the best parents possible and build the best marriage possible. It is imperative that the whole truth about marriage is told. The amazing blessing marriage can be for those who enter it according to God's design must be modeled. The dangers of a distorted view of marriage must also be clearly communicated.

# abnormality #3: same-sex marriage
## *(Redefining Marriage)*

In 1960 the idea of same-sex marriage was inconceivable in America. Now, the pressure to accept it as normative is increasing at an alarming rate. More and more states are adopting laws legalizing same-sex marriages. The Supreme Court has decided to leave the matter up to the states, thus opening up the door for public opinion, not common sense and human history, to sway the outcome.

Some will argue that it's not worth fretting over. Let same-sex couples marry. What difference does it make? Besides, it's inevitable so why make a big deal of it?  But it *is* a big deal—one that impacts the honor and sanctity of marriage as instituted by God, not to mention the religious liberty of Christians, Jews and other people of faith.

This is not a comfortable topic for most Christians to talk about. We know we will be labeled bigots because of our beliefs about marriage. But it must be talked about. Grandparents, we must not be forced into a *spiral of silence* on those issues that matter to God and impact the future of our families. It is important to understand all we can about this issue so we can speak to it intelligently…and compassionately.

We must know what the Word of God teaches so we will recognize the counterfeits and let the truth expose them for what they are. The legalization of same-sex marriage is happening because our culture has lost its mooring of truth. From the earliest records of human history to the present, marriage was understood to be a unique relationship and sacred institution established by God between a man and woman.

The current debate is an attempt to abolish all meaning from this sacred institution. Adam Mersereau is correct in his assessment of the motive behind the same-sex movement of the gay community. "Gay activists," he concludes, "claim to believe marriage is so meaningful that it should be extended to gays, but their case rests upon the belief that marriage is so meaningless that it can be claimed by anyone who wants it."[3]

Fortunately, there are those in the gay community who do not support same-sex marriage. They are few, but Doug Mainwaring is one of them. In an article written for *Public Discourse* he explains his reasons why same-sex marriage should be opposed.

> "The notion of same-sex marriage is implausible, yet political correctness has made stating the obvious a risky business. Genderless marriage is not marriage at all. It is something else entirely…To give kids two moms or two dads is to withhold from them someone whom they desperately need and deserve in order to be whole and happy. It is to permanently etch 'deprivation' on their hearts."[4]

Doug is right, and his position has earned him the scorn and wrath of the politically correct crowd. He does not argue from the point of view of faith or 'religion', but common sense alone. Yet, even he acknowledges that there are those who delight in "slowly chipping away at the bedrock of American culture: faith and family life." We better make sure we understand the consequences of eroding that bedrock. That means we need to seek more opportunities for public discourse on the matter.

On this issue, grandparents, a word to the wise. The position we take on this issue must be rooted in truth and compassion. If we are to engage in honest dialogue with our grandchildren's generation, they must know we care about them as much as we care about the truth. The biblical view of marriage and family is not popular in the halls of political correctness today. It is certain to earn you the hateful scorn of those who want to obliterate the truth. It will be you, however, who will be labeled *hate-monger*. Make sure there is no just cause for such an accusation that will hinder the truth from being heard or the beauty and sanctity of marriage from being visible.

Traditional marriage, in which there is a committed father and mother, is and always will be the only truly effective means for creating, nurturing, protecting, and educating children. Divorce, co-habitation and same-sex marriage all threaten this sacred institution. It is too important to ignore or to take lightly.

It is important to understand the faulty thinking that drives these abnormalities and attempts to make them 'normative' in our culture. Learn, ask questions, and know what you're talking about. Understanding, coupled with genuine love and compassion, opens up amazing opportunities for dialogue and discourse, especially in your own family. Many young people have simply never been presented with another view.

My daughter was recently talking with an eighteen-year-old girl who had grown up in a good home that did not talk much about faith or the Bible. As they talked about the issue of same-sex marriage, she showed her some things the Bible had to say about marriage. Her response may not be that uncommon among many of the younger generation. She said, "I've never heard that before. No one ever told me there was another point of view." If you don't talk about it, maybe no one else will either.

Besides those cultural abnormalities that directly impact marriage and family, there are a couple of others worth examining. They have to do with the value of life and the postmodern view of faith and religion.

In the next chapter we will look at how a culture of narcissism says "do what is right in your own eyes" and how that undermines core building blocks of a stable society.

# food for thought and discussion:

- Talk about what you think worldview means and why it is important.

- Describe your understanding of the post-modern worldview expressed by relativism. How does relativism line up with Romans 1:18-32?

- Do you agree with the impact that relativism has had on marriage and family? Why or why not?

- What are ways we can begin to create opportunities for gracious dialogue with our grandchildren and others on these issues?

# action step:

Read Nehemiah 4:14. What are ways you can begin to implement some of the ideas generated by question #4 and fight for your families. Pray about it and ask God to give you wisdom, compassion and resolve to do them according to His grace and for His glory.

# the idolatry of individualism

g r a n d p a u s e :
*The excessive individualism of secular Western culture*
*is fundamentally incompatible with the life community as depicted in Scripture.*
From Intergenerational Christian Formation by Allen and Ross[1]

A New York Times journalist wrote about Oprah Winfrey's interview with Reille Hunter, former mistress of Senator John Edwards and the mother of a child by Senator Edwards. Responding to questions from Oprah about the impact the affair had on Senator Edwards's wife, Ms. Hunter expressed no regret whatsoever. In fact, in her view it "was a necessary stage in Mr. Edwards's process of self-actualization." She went on to say, "I followed my heart, and I believe it was the right thing to do, which is weird…because I didn't make any commitment to Elizabeth [Mrs. Edwards]. I wasn't the one lying to her."[2]

In a relativistic worldview, moral standards are not rooted in God's fixed moral law. Rather, they are left to the whims of individual opinions and desires. We've seen the consequences of that in the cultural view of marriage and family. Relativism reveres individualism as supreme—and at an enormous cost to society.

As human beings we are driven by what is inside our hearts, and if our hearts are stuffed with greed, lust, selfishness, and self-gratification, there will be little, if any, motivation to consider what is right, let alone what is good for society.

This postmodern world has embraced a free-for-all approach to right and wrong leaving our children confused and disconnected from reality. We are living in a time when human obligation is rejected in favor of individual human rights dictated by how one feels. This gives birth to a society that is morally castrated and capable of egregious evil in which good is called evil and evil is called good.

We've seen the consequences of postmodern relativism as it impacts marriage and family. In this chapter and the next we'll look at two other outcomes of a worldview in which individualism is elevated to supreme status. These are not things we can merely shake off and say, "Oh, well. No harm done." These are of such magnitude that they become a curse upon society.

## devaluation of life

The same self-centered views of life that impact morality and family relationships also have a bearing upon how a society views and values life, and in particular, human life. Devoid of a biblical worldview that celebrates the Imago Dei stamped upon every human being, personal convenience (some call it 'choice') soon overrides all concerns about the dignity and sanctity of human life.

Darwinism, the crown jewel of postmodern philosophy, is diametrically opposed to the notion of a Creator and a purposeful creation. When life has no meaning or purpose, neither does it have any value. It's not hard to imagine the consequences of such a worldview if we stop long enough to think about it. These are consequences today's generation of grandparents had a part in creating. Therefore we must accept responsibility for them and seek God's wisdom to correct these wrongs. Here are two of the consequences we have allowed to shape our culture:

## a. utilitarian view of life

Abortion is at the center of the sanctity of life debate. Ronald Reagan drilled down to the core issue when he said, "The real question today is not when human life begins, but what is the value of human life…and whether that tiny human life has a God-given right to be protected by the law—the same right we have."[3] Modern science supplies ample evidence that the unborn child is alive, is a distinct individual, and is a member of the human species. The problem lies in the unwillingness of society to publicly discuss the meaning of the value of human life at any stage of life. This has enormous consequences for all of us well beyond the issues of abortion.

The questions President Reagan raised are the same questions that must be answered when any decision must be made about protecting life. The ultimate conclusion of the Darwinian point of view is to weigh the value of a human life purely on utilitarian terms. Whether we are talking about persons who are handicapped, the mentally impaired, or the elderly who can no longer care for themselves, the dignity and sanctity of life is at the heart of the Gospel and the truth that man is created in the image of his Creator.

Abraham Lincoln, addressing the issue of slavery, went right to the heart of all matters of human life when he said, "nothing stamped with the divine image and likeness was sent into the world to be trodden on."[4]

Unfortunately, most attempts at discourse on the value and sanctity of human life have been silenced through intimidation, and so human life continues to be trodden on. The question remains whether public discourse on this vital concern will remain off limits, or whether those with an unshakable belief in the Imago Dei will pursue ways to engage that discourse as courageously as Wilberforce did in his day.

Grandparents, though we may find the public square predominantly antagonistic to any such discussion, at lease most of our families still remain fertile fields for productive dialogue. Let the battle for truth and life begin on this front.

Speaking at the National Prayer Breakfast in 1994, Mother Teresa minced no words about the consequences for a society that fails to protect the sanctity of life in the womb:

> *I feel that the greatest destroyer of peace today is abortion, because it is a war against the child—a direct killing of the innocent child—murder by the mother herself. And if we accept that a mother can kill her own child, how can we tell other people not to kill another?...Any country that accepts abortion is not teaching the people to love, but to use any violence to get what they want."*[5]

Who will stand in the gap and demonstrate to the world what it looks like to live as persons made in the image of God—persons who value life and will not exploit it for their own ends? The ultimate conclusion of a society in which life is devalued is anarchy. The ultimate outcome of anarchy—rampant violence where men look more like brute animals than the Imago Dei.

## b. rampant violence

Growing up in the Rocky Mountain region, I knew nothing as a child of the fears today's children and their parents face on a daily basis. My friends and I roamed freely in our neighborhoods without any concern by our parents. We walked a considerable distance to school each day without any worries about predators. Our parents thought nothing about us riding our bikes across town to play in a park or wander out on the prairie (you had to live there to understand).

Most of us born before 1960 probably enjoyed a similar environment growing up. School shootings, drug dealing, or teen suicides were not on our radar screen. The biggest issue we faced was probably getting caught chewing gum in class, or sneaking cigarettes behind the school building at recess. The only violence we dealt with was the occasional bully calling someone out after school to fight.

The world our children live in today is much different. Both children and parents are haunted by a dark shadow of societal paranoia spawned by out-of-control violence. Here are just a few new realities that have created so much paranoia among us today:

- Concern about school shootings and violence in any public place.

- Worry about child molesters in our neighborhoods, schools, athletic organizations and churches. We have to teach them to watch out for strangers. Background checks and child predator evaluations are normal in any formal program involving children.

- Tighten security checks that have taken the joy out of travel or gathering in major public events.

- Fear of terrorist bombings or weapons of mass destruction are constantly in the news both internationally and domestically.

- Spreading gang violence and violent crime in rural areas as well as big cities.

Sadly, we live in constant fear as a society. Why should it be otherwise when we tell our kids that human life has little value or meaning? Hope has been replaced with despair. We have a daunting task before us to change this reality so that our grandchildren can live Life with a capital 'L'—life filled with hope, purpose and joy in the midst of a turbulent world. Only Christ can offer that kind of life.

The call is going out for courageous grandparents who will face the challenges of bringing God's shalom into a world filled with fear, anxiety, and uncertainty. This generation is desperate for courageous saints who understand the truth and know what to do. Nehemiah was such a man in his day.

In the midst of opposition and fear, Nehemiah did the one thing that had always guided his life. He prayed to the God who made man in His image! Then he got off his knees confident in God's power, surveyed the situation with the eyes of wisdom, and developed a plan that probably seemed crazy to many.

Confident in God's ability to do the impossible, he stood before a fearful people and gave them a reason to hope. They did not need to fear, he told them, because "our God will fight for us" (Neh. 4:20)! Nehemiah understood what was going on. He also knew what God wanted him to do, and he did it.

It does not require a seminary degree or a PhD to figure out what God wants you to do as well. He asks you to trust Him because you are His workmanship— His masterpiece. He asks you to believe that He has already equipped you for His purpose for your life. But He does not ask you to engage with that purpose alone. He has placed you in a family—the body of Christ.

Unfortunately, many of us have bought into another lie that prevents us from realizing that purpose. It is the supremacy of *individualism*, which not only impacts marriage and family and the sanctity and value of life, but our view of faith and community.

## devaluation of community

Individualism shapes not only how we approach religion or faith but also how we do life together. Let's briefly look into each of these cultural perceptions to better understand the societal dynamic rooted in an individualistic worldview.

# designer religion

Writing for *USA Today*, Cathy Lynn Grossman, quotes George Barna: "We are a designer society. We want everything customized to our personal needs—our clothing, our food, our education. Now it's our religion."[6] Perhaps you remember the Burger King slogan: *Have It Your Way!* This is the way of religious faith in America. The dominance of individualism has radically infected people's approach and attitude towards religion and spirituality.

People pick and choose what they want from the religious smorgasbord at their fingertips. At the postmodern buffet you can pick whatever makes sense to you: "I'll have a little belief in God, as long as He doesn't interfere with what I want to do. Some Bible will be fine, but only the tasty portions, if you please. I'll take some grace, but leave off the repentance, please. Oh, let's see, I'll have a little Jesus with some Eastern mysticism thrown in for dessert."

In many American evangelical churches, this consumer-oriented philosophy is catered to with modern marketing techniques. Topics about sin, repentance, obedience, and self-denial are avoided in favor of large doses of grace, forgiveness, happiness, and love. Don't get me wrong—I cherish these sacred truths because they are at the heart of the Gospel. My concern is the employment of them to make people feel good at the expense of their souls. When only part of the truth is taught, the Gospel is stripped of its full meaning and transformational power.

Stan Guthrie, author of *All That Jesus Asks*, makes it clear that Jesus is not an action figure purchased at Wal-Mart who is "infinitely bendable, able to assume whatever postmodern pose we give Him."[7] We can't pick and choose what we want to believe. God is the standard for truth, not man.

Speaking the truth is not popular. Truth is often unpleasant, but it is also life-giving. Grandparents have a responsibility to sit at the city gates of our families and society to serve as gatekeepers of truth for the next generations.

# designer community relationships

The family Thanksgiving dinner was finished and the plates cleared. The adults sat at the table sharing opinions about current events of the day. Fourteen-year-old Chad remained at the table as the adults talked and listened with interest. When he offered his opinion on the subject, his mother turned to him and said, "Just go out with the rest of the kids, Chad. This is an adult conversation."

As we have already seen, North America has embraced the practice of emphasizing individual generations above the larger inter-generational family or community. We even identify these groups with generation-specific labels like Boomers, GenX'rs, Mosaics, and so forth. It's as though our capacity to think and process life in the context of a whole community has diminished significantly. *This generation*—all the generations living at a given time—has been replaced *my generation* or *that generation* terminology.

The upshot of this mindset is the acceptance of our current generational disconnection as something normative. After all, everything is a matter of individual preference, and so the past has little to do with the present. Yet without a narrative that expresses who we are, why we are here, and how we should relate to each other and our Creator, the generation gap only continues to widen…at a very high cost to all.

Happily there is a growing sense among many young adults that something has indeed been lost without an historical truth narrative. They may not know what that means, but deep down they know that our *rights-driven* culture in which the individual is elevated over the community somehow feels out of sync.

Even the church—one of the few places in our culture where ALL the generations come together in one place at one time—offers little clarity. As our families walk in the door of the church, the generations immediately separate into 'life-stages' or 'departments' with little or no meaningful interaction between them. The church may be *multi*-generational, but it is far from *inter*-generational!

I believe God established and ordained a *truth narrative* from which each of the generations live with, learn from, and give to one another as a family. Psalm 78 describes the responsibility of parents and grandparents to tell the next generations God's story because it matters to all of us. This biblical idea of family and the body of Christ is at the heart of this narrative.

Grandparents must lead the charge toward restoring an inter-generational culture, first in our families, but also in our churches. This is what it means to live a legacy that outlives us. It's more than telling the story of God's amazing work. It's doing so in the context of the generations engaging with that story together. Psalm 145 says, *"one generation will commend your work to another…"* We each have something important to share with each other—older to younger, and younger to older. I'll deal with this more in chapter 15, "Leaving a Well-Versed Legacy."

For now, let me say this. Grandparents, we have an opportunity to change the culture. It starts with our own families. Be careful about the 'two-table' mentality when our families gather for important events like Thanksgiving or Christmas dinners and any other family gathering. You know the model—the adult table in one place, the kids' table in another. Look for every opportunity to engage with your grandchildren and their parents about the important issues of life, not separate each other.

One of my favorite TV programs is *Blue Bloods*. I enjoy the interaction of various members of the Reagan family as they play out their roles in the New York police department and DA's office. But what I love most is the scene in every episode when four generations of Reagans sit around the dinner table and talk about life together. Great-Grandpa, Grandpa, parents, children—each is included the conversation and everyone's input and questions are valued. It's a wonderful picture of inter-generational relationships, and sadly, a stark contrast to most families today.

The patriarchs, prophets, apostles and our Lord Himself used the term *this generation* to speak of a connectedness and shared life that blesses and benefits everyone of every age, not just a single generation. I believe most of us long for that meaningful re-engagement for this generation as well. We have settled too long for the lie of individualism and generational separatism.

Now is the time for courageous grandparents everywhere to step to the plate and intentionally live out this foundational truth designed to bless us all: *From him [Christ] the <u>whole body</u>, joined and held together by every supporting ligament, grows and builds itself up in love, <u>as each part does its work</u>* (Ephesians 4:16).

# food for thought and discussion:

- Read Proverbs 16:25. How does this relate to the issues discussed in this chapter?

- In what ways does individualism shape our understanding today of the value of life and the meaning of the body of Christ as found in Scripture? (Here are some texts you might want to examine: Genesis 1:27-31; 5:1-2; Psalm 8:3-9; 139:1-16; Romans 12:1-13; I Corinthians 12:12-27; Ephesians 4:1-16; I Peter 2:4-10)

- What is the difference between multi-generational and inter-generational? Which do you think most accurately describes our families and churches in America today? Why?

- How can we counter the negative effects of individualism and generational separatism in our day and in our culture?

# action step:

What will you change in the way you look at life and family to more accurately represent the value God places on life and His body? Read Luke 10:23-37 (Good Samaritan). Ask God to show you how to put that in practice this week.

# repristinators or reposers

### g r a n d p a u s e :

*"We are the salt of the earth, not the sugar, and our ministry is truly to cleanse and not just to change the taste."*

Vance Havner

**M**y grandparents used to have a white picket fence across the front yard of their house. I loved that picket fence. I remember a few years after Grandpa had passed away, that white picket fence began to look a little worse for wear. The paint was peeling and some of the pickets had cracked or were broken. That's what happens when something is left to the natural process of deterioration.

Then one day my father came to the house with a hammer and a bucket of white paint. Before long that while picket fence looked like it was supposed to look—a bright, cheery adornment for Grandma's front yard. It had been *repristinated*—restored to its original condition!

Perhaps that's not a word you have heard before, but it is a legitimate word. According to Webster's, to *repristinate* is "to restore something to its original state or condition." I can't help but believe that one of the roles God has given grandparents is to be *repristinators* (that's my word). We have been given the understanding and tools to restore the worse-for-wear culture we helped created back to its original condition according to God's design. Or we could choose to be *reposers* (my word again), who lie around like we're dead and do nothing.

Our worldview determines what we perceive as valid and valued and will ultimately move us to be either *reprisinators* or *reposers*. History suggests that if at least 10 percent of the members of a society hold an unshakable belief in something, the majority of that society will also embrace that belief. The kind of unshakable belief that influences a society or culture with such power involves more than holding a personal opinion about something. Unshakable belief is a deep and unalterable conviction embodied in a visible way of doing life. It is so vibrant that it catches the attention of the culture in which we live. It's called *repristination*.

As followers of Christ we hold an unalterable conviction that God is, that He created us for Himself, and that He has paid the ultimate price to restore man to a personal relationship with his Creator and escape the judgment that would otherwise be inescapable. Our unshakable faith in God's truth is the basis for wisdom to understand the times. It compels us to compassionately act upon that wisdom in the power of the Holy Spirit to draw others to Christ and His salvation.

Christ commanded us to make disciples worldwide who follow Christ with the same unshakable commitment. That is what the Great Commission is about. There is more, however, to the proclamation of the Gospel than the words we speak. If the words we speak are not validated by an authentic demonstration of the transforming, life-giving power of the Gospel in the way we live, the rest of the world will remain unaffected by it. That pretty much describes the way of a reposer.

Chuck Colson suggests that concurrent with the Great Commission we are also called to fulfill what he calls the Cultural Commission.[1] It is another way of saying that God calls us to more than the proclamation of the Gospel.

According to Genesis 1:27-28, we are called to live as redemptive agents who, made in the image of God, rule, produce, reproduce, and steward the earth. We were reborn to that purpose through the Gospel. The Gospel must not be reduced to little more than a free ticket to heaven.

As Colson suggests, Christ's disciples are also commissioned to serve as God's agents in "sustaining and renewing creation, defending the created institutions of family and society, and exposing false worldviews."[2] In other words, the new birth is but the starting point for true disciples, albeit the critical and essential starting point. Indeed, it is the miracle of a new life that compels Christ's disciples to engage the world with the whole truth and make disciples who do the same.

Jesus came to testify to the truth. We are to do the same. While defending, proclaiming, and authenticating the Truth exposes the Lie, I am convinced that no amount of reason or carefully crafted persuasion will engage the world and cause it to change. It is the incarnation of truth by people of unshakable faith that will open the door for the Holy Spirit to convict the world.

Such unshakable faith is displayed where we live and work in the marketplace, the laboratory, the classroom, the neighborhood, and the home. If we are to be effective agents of change, our lives must display the glory of what should be. Only then will the Holy Spirit work through us to transform and re-make our culture. Nice theology, but what does it mean?

# culture 101

Let's begin by defining what we mean when we use the word *culture*. Here's a crash course in Culture 101 that I hope will be useful. Andy Crouch uses the term *culture-making* in his book by the same title to describe how culture is changed or created. He suggests that we often misuse the word *culture* as a one-size-fits-all description of our society. In reality, society is made up of many cultures formed around geography, ethnicity, family structures and traditions, religion or faith, and specific *cultural goods* that characterize that culture.

In other words, no singular culture exists which describes every person or place in a particular country, city, or neighborhood. Any talk about American culture is actually a discussion about many different cultures. While Crouch states that there is no such thing as 'the Culture,' he argues, "finding our place in the world as culture makers requires us to pay attention to culture's many dimensions."[3] So, how are we to accurately understand it?

Culture is story. It is the story of man who, created in the image of God, is working to create his story in the context of God's larger story. Stated more succinctly, culture is what we make of the world, both in terms of what we do or create with what we have been given, as well as how we interpret and express the mystery and wonder of our world.

Isaac Newton, for example, completely reshaped the culture of the scientific world as a result of his work. His understanding of God as Creator of a universe established with natural laws led him to develop his theory of gravitation and three laws of motion. His work was the result of his observations of the wonder of God's design. He took what he observed, validated it, and compiled a new way of seeing our world and how it works that had never been done before. The Scientific Revolution was born because one man took what he had been given in this world and made something of it.

But what happens when culture goes awry, as it often does? Is it possible to transform it? Again, Crouch suggests that attempts to transform culture are largely misguided. He argues that we are not called to transform but to make or create culture to supplant or replace an existing one. Thus, while it is important to understand the culture or cultures in which we live, when it comes to changing it, we must first understand the culture God expects *us* to make in the first place. (By the way, Crouch also calls attention to the fact that family is the basic unit of culture—"culture at its smallest and most powerful." Strong families serve as a primary staging area for engaging culture and making something of it.)

Changing culture is little more than the process of introducing something that the majority of society will embrace in exchange for what they already have. In other words, if we are to change culture, we will have to offer something that others in that culture are persuaded is better than what they have.

Attempts at changing culture fail because of a faulty understanding of how culture is made. Crouch identifies three *postures* that actually hinder the process of changing, or more accurately, making culture. I have added a fourth. These are the postures of *reposers*, and it is unlikely they will make any headway as a positive force for the re-making of currently established cultural norms.

> *1. Condemning culture:* My wife and I love to fix ham hocks and pinto beans with cornbread on a cold day. It has been part of our family culture for at least two generations. My grandkids, on the other hand, are not so crazy about beans and cornbread, even when it's smothered with ketchup (yummy!). However, no amount of sarcastic condemnation by the

grandkids or our in-laws aimed at our beans and cornbread feast is going to change our tradition as long as we're living.

The same is true for any culture. If the only thing we do is condemn a particular cultural good or tradition, we are likely to produce no positive impact for change whatsoever. Rarely will anyone give up something unless something better is offered to take its place. Take television for example. We can sit around condemning the programs on television all we want, but the financial incentives of television producers is too strong to change what they do simply because a group of people condemn it. Unless a better alternative with equally viable economic benefits is offered, television programming will go on as it is—constantly deteriorating.

*2. Critiquing culture:* Crouch argues that a more subtle approach of analysis and critique rarely affects culture either. More education produces the same non-effect. Just because someone receives a carefully crafted analysis of all the fallacies and benefits of a thing doesn't mean that thing will change significantly. In fact, the likelihood it will produce long-term change is slim to none. My grandkids may come upon with a nutritional analysis of our cornbread and beans with facts about how unhealthy it might be, but it won't change our tradition. Again, change can only be affected when something new and better is offered in its place, and so far none of our grandkids have presented a better alternative to our cornbread and beans.

*3. Copying culture:* In America we have attempted to create a Christian subculture that offers 'alternatives' to certain cultural goods. Christian television networks have surfaced in an attempt to imitate the general public market, hoping to offer a more palatable product. The music industry has also taken this approach. Crouch argues that while these may be good for a particular subculture, they have no real impact on the general public's television or music culture. "Any cultural good, after all, only moves the horizons for the particular public who experience it," he observes. "For the rest of the world, it is as if that piece of culture, no matter how excellent or significant it may be, never existed… When we copy culture within our own private enclaves, the culture at large remains unchanged."[4] Copy-cat cultures have little impact on the rest of the world.

*4. Ignoring culture:* You've probably heard someone say, "Oh, just ignore it. It'll go away on its own." Culture may seem to morph or re-create itself over time, but it never does so without someone introducing the change. The cultures around us are formed by deliberate, intentional means by those who have the power to influence what is valued.

Sitting in silence only allows another group of people to determine what culture or cultures are going to dominate our society. Our grandkids can sit in silence and refuse to eat our cornbread and beans. However, it will still be served because those of us who like it are in a position to keep it going. It will remain as a valued family ritual until another generation goes into the kitchen and creates a new cultural tradition to take its place.

Understanding the culture around us is the first step towards impacting our world. If you want to understand the culture we live in you need understand something about one the great culture shapers of our time—technology. The next section unpacks some basic concepts that will help us untangle this complex technological web we have woven.

Once again you must decide whether you will approach this subject as a *repristinator* or a *reposer*. Repristinators want to understand so they know what to do. Reposers don't care.

You must decide which you will be.

# food for thought and discussion:

- What is the difference between a *repristinator* and a *reposer*? Which would your grandchildren or adult children say you are? Which would *you* say that you are?

- What is culture? How is culture shaped or created? What prevents us from making a positive impact on shaping or re-making culture?

- What do you understand to be the difference between the Great Commission and the 'Cultural Commission'?

# action steps:

If you want to be a repristinator-type person who will positively impact change in our culture, I recommend the following resources to help you understand how to do that. I urge you to get copies and read them. Here are my recommendations:

- Daniel, Chapter 1; As an example of how four young men lived in, but not of, the culture thrust upon them, this gives me hope for future generations. It is also a great reminder to those of us who are older of how God can use anyone who wants to be a *repristinator* and not a *reposer*.

- *You Lost Me: Why Young Christians Are Leaving Church…And Rethinking Faith* by David Kinnaman, Baker Books, 2011.

- *Coffee Shop Conversations: Making the Most of Spiritual Small Talk* by Dale and Jonalyn Fincher, Zondervan, 2010.

# p a r t   t h r e e

# SIZE UP!

*I went to Jerusalem, and after staying there three days I set out during the night with a few men. I had not told anyone what my God had put in my heart to do for Jerusalem. There were no mounts with me except the one I was riding on.*

*By night I went out through the Valley Gate toward the Jackal Well and the Dung Gate, examining the walls of Jerusalem, which had been broken down, and its gates, which had been destroyed by fire… The officials did not know where I had gone or what I was doing, because as yet I had said nothing to the Jews or the priests or nobles or officials or any others who would be doing the work.*

*Then I said to them, "You see the trouble we are in: Jerusalem lies in ruins, and its gates have been burned with fire. Come, let us rebuild the wall of Jerusalem, and we will no longer be in disgrace." I also told them about the gracious hand of my God upon me and what the king had said to me.*

*They replied, "Let us start rebuilding." So they began this good work.*

Excerpted from Nehemiah 2:1-18 (NIV)

# untangling the technology web!

Tom and Betty looked forward to celebrating Thanksgiving with their daughter and her family who lived across the country. They eagerly looked forward to this overdue reunion. There would be so much to catch up on—so much to share about all the blessings God had poured into their family since the last time they saw each other. With only a few precious days to enjoy with their family, Tom and Betty did not want to waste a single moment. They decided to turn off their computer, TV, and cell phones so nothing would interfere with the few precious days they had together.

When the moment finally arrived, the much-anticipated union was welcomed with a deluge of unrestrained hugs and kisses. Within moments of this grand gathering, before the last hug was discharged or coats were hung up, a cacophony of beeps, dings, and obnoxious tunes disrupted their cherished reunion. Calls and text messages regularly interrupted their conversations. Apparently, Mom, Dad and the kids did not get the memo about Tom and Betty's desire for a distraction-free visit.

At the dinner table the grandkids continued to send and receive text messages with their friends. One grandchild came to the table with his iPod earphones stuffed in his ears, tuned out to any conversations that might occur. Tom and Betty were understandably disappointed and upset. Does it sound familiar?

An unwanted visitor intruded upon their family gathering and robbed them of the meaningful personal exchanges they had anticipated. Technology had significantly and unexpectedly reshaped how their family interacted. The Norman Rockwell image of family enjoying each other and sharing life had degenerated into a family alone together, and they did not know what to do about it.

In a day when families once lived and worked side by side on the family farm, individual family members shared a common task and purpose that typically linked them in a tight-knit community. Technology has entangled personal and work life with never-ending links to outsiders via smart phones, email, and Facebook. These technological wonders can hinder the binding of relationships because virtual conversations replace shared endeavors.

In fact, Christine Rosen, senior editor of *The New Atlantis*, believes the constant virtual connections created by technology often disrupt shared endeavors. She explains, "What family members do around each other at home has less and less to do with each other… Every public space is now potentially a scene for the private if we can reach out to those we know via technology."[1] How are we to respond to this technological intrusion upon personal relationships, especially family relationships?

Everything about our lives has been dramatically impacted by technology, particularly media technologies. High definition television, computers, DVRs, iPods, iPads, e-books, cell phones, and now smart phones are as commonplace in our world as roads and highways. With the exception of television and a few personal computers, most of these never existed or were not available to the general public before 1990. These new technological highways have completely changed the landscape of our lives. It's like watching a paranoid chameleon trying to adapt to a constantly changing technological environment.

Who would have imagined fifty years ago that almost every person in America would carry a cell phone connecting him or her with almost anyone in the world? In 1960 who would have believed that everyone would someday have his or her own personal computer—more than one in many cases? Few of us envisioned devices called smart phones or iPads or notebooks that would allow us to carry our personal computer with us anywhere we go. Cars that perform functions by voice-activation or park themselves with hands-off steering were things only imagined in sci-fi films and comic books.

The truth is we aren't in Kansas anymore—or even Oz. Our world is now a technologically dependent world. Things will never be the same. Who knows what new technologies will emerge to change the landscape again in the next few years? This is the age of technology. We would be foolish to ignore it. It is important to understand what is going on in this technological age.

Spring Keepers understand that technology is here to stay, but they care about minimizing the polluting effects of technology in our lives. We recognize that left unchecked and uncontrolled technology will wreak havoc in our lives.

Right now you may be wondering if anything can be done other than sit back and watch it happen. It's all too overwhelming. Technology seems to have a life of its own. Sometimes it feels like we're on a runaway train without an engineer heading for a wide, deep canyon, and the bridge is out. How do we stop the train?

Perhaps you are one of the few people who don't really care. You resist having anything to do with the new technologies. You don't give a hoot about computers, email, or Skype. If you have a cell phone, you prefer a 'dumb' phone over a 'smart' phone. You want no part of Facebook or Twitter and see no reason to learn how to text. You don't know an app from a tweet and don't want to know. You have *tech-apathy* and are content to be a *tech-dummy*.

On the other hand, if you are a grandparent age sixty-five or younger, you probably already have several of the latest tech-gadgets. You keep in touch with your grandchildren through email, texting, Skype, and you are actively connected on Facebook and Twitter. You may be tech-savvy, but have you taken time away from the tech stuff long enough to evaluate and understand the dangers you embrace?

Perhaps you fall somewhere in between, not quite sure just how much technology you should embrace, and a little uncertain about getting too caught up in the technological frenzy. You are tech-wary because you are tech-aware. You recognize the dangers and are concerned about how much is too much.

Wherever you are in the spectrum of technology comprehension, personal use, or level of comfort, I recommend that you make an effort to know something about what is going on even if you aren't going to use it. Disciplined discernment is required. If you want to help your children and grandchildren use it well, you'd better know something about it yourself.

Now, before you roll your eyes and put down the book, I ask you to read on and not give up yet. You don't have to be a geek to figure out a technological game plan.

## grandparenting in a digital world

Many of the older generation are fond of proclaiming how they got along just fine without any of this new technology. They feel it has all cheapened the quality of life and added unnecessary complexity to our lives. You can often hear them complain about it and criticize all the new-fangled gadgets they don't understand.

Whether you are tech-savvy or not, the chances are your grandchildren are. If the only thing they hear from you is complaints and tirades about the evils of technology, then the opportunity for meaningful dialogue will essentially shut down. On the other hand, expressing a willingness to genuinely engage their world and make an attempt to understand it will put you in a position to be able speak into their world at some point. So, before you rush out and enroll in a computer class or sign up for a course on some of the newest technologies, here are a few principles that will help lay a solid foundation:

- **God is the creator of technology.** He created our brains and all the elements and laws of nature that allow technology to work the way it does. Made in God's image, we are creators by nature, made to create and be creative. Technology is a logical result of man's creativity and God's creative genius in the things He has made. So, whether we are talking about cars or computers, heating pads or iPads, technology exists because God created a world where man has unlimited possibilities for expressing his creativity.

- **Technology is not inherently evil or sinful—we are**. Technology can be used for good or evil. If there are abuses and wrongful uses, it is because we are by nature sinners prone to use good for evil. Unfortunately, too many well-meaning Christians are quick to pounce on newer technological creations and denounce them as inherently evil. Television, movies, the internet are examples of technologies that have been condemned as evil. Technological creations are not by nature evil, but they are often instruments through which evil and corrupt purposes are promoted.

  The same was true for the printing press. Shall we throw out all books as evil and sinful because there are authors who use them for such purposes? How about the light bulb, or the typewriter…or curling irons? Where shall we draw the line between what is good and what is not? Attempts to do that often result in even more evil.

  Technology is a neutral, inanimate, soul-less thing. How we use it and how we view it determine whether it becomes an instrument for good and the glory of our Creator or an instrument of harm and destruction. All the dangers of technology that we will explore are rooted in the sin nature.

- **Technology can be used for good**. There are plenty of good uses for the technologies men create. We must pay attention to the dangers, but if that is all we do, we will miss the possibilities for making use of these things as instruments of good. Dr. David Murray, Professor of Practical Theology at Puritan Reformed Theological Seminary, produced a video that can be used to help train children to use *disciplined discernment* in the proper use of technology for the glory of God and for their own good.[2] Our goal should be to help them avoid the pitfalls of technology and to make wise choices in the use of it.

It is not possible to examine all the technologies of our day in a book like this. For our purposes we will discuss some of the prominent media technologies currently on the market—technologies your grandchildren most likely often use. We'll examine these, briefly highlighting the traps they impose, the vigilance necessary to counter those traps, and the opportunities media technology presents for blessing others.

## digital idolatry

The constant flow of new technologies and applications prey upon our greed and the need to keep up with the Joneses. We are deluded into thinking that the latest technologies are must-have items. We are afraid of becoming obsolete, so the continual deluge of deceptive marketing messages tell us how important it is to keep up with the latest tools (toys) so our lives will be easier and better. Apple has mastered the marketing message as well as anyone.

We have bought into the lie that we have to have it now. People stand in long lines the night before the newest version of the latest iPad or iPhone is released to be one of the first to have it. Once we have it, we are consumed by it and the need to continually upgrade for more speed, a larger selection of apps, and more features.

Other technologies such as Xbox video game systems, Wii, smart phones, YouTube, and social networking consume young and old alike. Greed and the lust for more dictate our impulsive buying habits and consuming addictions. We are easily lured into making technology an idol in our life. Acquiring disciplined discernment rooted in godly wisdom and virtue will keep us from being caught in the deceptive traps of technology.

Disciplined discernment is applying the *understanding-the-times* portion of the Issachar principle. Do you remember Tom and Betty? Put yourself in their situation. Besides being miffed that your kids and grandkids are not paying enough attention to you, there is a danger of allowing technology to control lives without any boundaries. How would you handle their situation? Would you write off the whole matter as something not important enough to deal with, or would you take a hard stand on the matter?

Disciplined discernment is not just being annoyed at something, nor is it burying your head in the sand and pretending it doesn't matter. Discernment is the ability to identify the real danger—in this case the destruction of meaningful community and genuine relational intimacy that happens best through face-to-face communication. The loss of intimacy does not contribute to healthy family relationships. It disconnects families and undermines personal relationships. It is a new form of idolatry that can grip us if we are not careful and wise.

In the next section we continue our exploration of this digital world. We will size up our culture and the various technology traps that need to be avoided. We'll examine some due diligence principles that will help you be an effective change agent in your grandchildren's lives. We'll also size up the attitudes— whether as a *repristinator* or a *reposer*—that may determine your impact as you engage the culture.

# food for thought and discussion:

- Do you agree with the three principles of technology? Why or why not?

- In what ways has technology become a source of idolatry today? Can you cite any examples in your own life, family or friendships that illustrate this?

- What is your feeling about today's technology? How are you dealing with it? Is your attitude providing a good example or causing some level of alienation for your grandchildren?

# action step:

Make the decision to intentionally learn what you can about today's technologies (you don't nee to be an expert). Look over the technology resources listed in Appendix 1. Pick one or two that could help you become more knowledgeable on this subject and give you more opportunities to talk with your grandchildren without appearing out of touch.

# avoiding technology's traps

*"Our imaginations are what help us change the world."*
Shane Hipps, author of *Flickering Pixels*

**N**ot only is idolatry a potential trap, there are other very dangerous technology traps that must be understood for what they are. It is tempting for grandparents to overlook these things and not say much in order to appease the grandchildren, especially if they aren't into technology that much. After all, who doesn't want their grandkids to like them? So it might be tempting to look the other way and not address these issues. That would be a mistake. Why? Because this is a critical area where the souls of our grandchildren are at stake.

Some grandparents rationalize that the *parents* are responsible for dealing with these matters, so they won't get involved. That's another lie—or a cop out. Never lose sight of the importance of the partnership that should exist between parents and grandparents. When that partnership is working in harmony, we can work together to help our grandchildren avoid these traps.

Diligence in our own lives and in the way we use technology is also required in order to set an example for our grandchildren of what it looks like to live Life (with a capital 'L') in Christ free from the bondage of technology.

Let's examine four potential technology traps against which we need to keep ourselves alert and diligent:

## trap #1: death by amusement

Author Neil Postman wrote that the real threat to society is not a Big Brother oppressor but people who choose to "adore the technologies that undo their capacities to think."[1] Our word *amuse* comes from the root *muse* which means "to think." The negative prefix 'a' is added to the word to negate the original meaning of the root word. Thus, *amuse* means "not to think." As Mark Hamby, president and founder of Lamplighter Publishing observes, "Technology and media have become amusements that sedate us into a hypnotic state."[2]

Inattention is one of the great consequences of amusement technology in the modern world. The amusement assault in this age of technological communication has made focused attention on important issues and matters of life nearly nonexistent. The ability to focus one's attention enough to think critically and sensibly is almost as rare as a politician keeping a campaign promise. Sound bites and rapid-fire commentaries diminish our ability to ponder anything substantive. That is a huge potential trap that courageous grandparents must be on the look out for.

Amusement in the form of entertainment is the focus of much of today's technology. It can literally consume almost every waking hour. Constant entertainment immersion via TV, video and online games, texting, Facebook, and internet apps leaves little time for opportunities that build character and develop imagination. What a child repeatedly sees and hears determines what that child will retain, how that child will think or not think, and what values he will embrace. Sesame Street taught children to love school, but only if it entertains like Sesame Street.

According to a 2010 article in the *New York Times*, the more a child is bombarded with the various media stimuli of our culture, the more their brains are literally rewired to think in illogical and disconnected thought patterns making them "more habituated…to constantly switching tasks—and less able to sustain attention."[3] That's because extensive media exposure rewires brain activity to the right side where incoming messages are not analyzed by logic, but by emotion—the heart of entertainment. This results in the child's emotional feelings influencing his responses rather than critical thinking and evaluation. By contrast, the brain of a child who does a lot of reading or is read to frequently develops the ability to think logically and critically—a left-side function.

Flash mobs are an example of the dangerous and destructive activities generated through social networks where logic and critical thinking are nonexistent. There are plenty of charlatans in our world who understand how the brain can be manipulated to bypass all critical analysis and sound reasoning when it is engaged at an emotional level. Media technology, when not checked by truth and critical discernment, is a dangerous trap with potentially devastating consequences to individuals and society.

It's not hard to imagine how this 'rewiring' of the brain can also impact a child's ability to process matters of faith and truth. When confronted with the explosion of ideas and unfiltered opinions that pass through the digital network constantly, an inability to think critically leads to instability and emotional reactions without substance. This person looks for that which makes him feel good. James says such a person is like the *"wave of the sea, blown and tossed by the wind…he is a double-minded man, unstable in all he does"* (James 1:6, 8).

Contrasting the two renowned works of George Orwell's *1984* and Andrew Huxley's *Brave New World*, author Neil Postman again wrote: "Orwell feared that what we hate will ruin us. Huxley feared that what we love will ruin us."[4] May God grant us the wisdom to hate evil and love the truth and know how to teach our children and grandchildren to so the same.

# taking the 'a' out of amusement

What can you do to keep your grandchild's mind engaged? Here are a few suggestions.

- Make time to read to your grandchildren rather than allowing them to sit in front of a TV or computer. Read books that will engage their imaginations and draw them into the story. I have a reading list in the Appendix that you might find helpful.

- Challenge your grandkids to a reading contest. Prepare a reading list that you have already approved and ask them to choose books or articles from that list to read over the next month. Offer a special prize (maybe a day at the zoo or a theme park, or maybe a dinner and movie night out) for reading a predetermined number of pages in that month. Make the challenge once a quarter or three times a year at most. If you are long distance, you can tally points that can be used however you decide to use them. Be creative—you have it in you to make it happen.

- Plan a game night with your grandkids if they are nearby or when they come to visit. Set up several game options that everyone can play, and have them rotate from one game to the next. When the timer goes off, everyone moves and resumes playing wherever the previous players left off.

- Propose a tech-fast challenge for twenty-four hours. No TV, cell phones, emails, computer games, Wii, etc. for a whole day (or whatever period of time you choose). Ask everyone to write down what they did during that time. Did they learn anything they might not have learned if they had been connected to their technology toys? What was the hardest part?

## trap #2: virtual unreality

My cousin told me about a friend of his, a grandfather, who spent a special evening on the town with his grandson. They went to dinner and a movie together, but during the entire evening his grandson rarely stopped texting on his cell phone, even during the movie. Irritated, the grandfather was tempted to grab the cell phone and give his grandson a good lecture about basic politeness, but he restrained himself. When the evening was over, he decided instead to ask this question: "I'm going to ask you a question," he said, "and I want you to think about it. We'll talk about it later. Do you think you were you with me tonight in our time together?"

The grandfather dropped him off at home and let him ponder his question. Because his grandson respected his grandfather and knew him to be a man of honor and integrity, he went home and gave it some thought. He even began a conversation with the rest of his family who were just as guilty of habitual texting.

The next week he apologized to his grandfather for his rudeness while they were together. He made a pledge to be more sensitive to appropriate uses of his cell phone. They were able to talk freely about the importance of relationships, what it means to be with someone, and how to manage modern technologies like cell phones so that they don't interfere with honoring others.

Virtual reality, the engaging of a person's mind with an imaginary reality, has long been part of human existence through theater and the arts. Modern technology has opened up a whole new world of virtual reality in which a person can enter an artificially simulated environment generated by computers. Now, for the first time, computers and cell phones have propelled us into yet another arena of virtual relationships. Mark Hamby calls this phenomenon *virtual unreality*. Virtual unreality is the substitution of online virtual connections for real face-to-face relationships. It produces an inability to express simple social skills and courtesies due to obsessive, undisciplined uses of technology in social settings.

The trap of virtual unreality is that social technology tools such as texting and social networking are so easy to get hooked on. Without even realizing it, a person will find himself addicted and substituting virtual friendships for genuine face-to-face relationships. 'Friends' are now only a click away.

According to a study conducted by a neuroscience group at the University of Southern California, social networking sites like Twitter and Facebook "fail to provide a place to feel compassion or even admiration."[5] While it is not uncommon for people to have hundreds and even thousands of 'friends' on Facebook, these are mostly mile-wide and inch-deep friendships—a far cry from the reality of true friendships.

A recent car commercial helps put it in perspective. It shows a teenage girl sitting at a computer commenting about how her parents are missing out on *life* because they only have sixteen *friends* on Facebook instead of the hundreds she has. As she talks, the scene switches to her parents biking with friends and enjoying life in the outdoors. The scene jumps back to the daughter at her computer as she posts and reads posts from her online 'friends' saying, "This is living." The scene switches back to the parents loading their bikes onto their new car.

Sadly, virtual unreality is an illusion many foolishly embrace. While the commercial portrays the parents as really 'getting it' when it comes to living a full life, I have to wonder what the parents are doing to help their daughter 'get it' too

(I know, it's only a commercial). But the sad truth is that many parents are not helping their kids 'get it'. They have left them to figure out life and relationships on their own with technology as their mentor. Grandparents, don't be guilty of the same mistake.

In an earlier *USA Today* article, Mark Vernon says that close friends "sit with one another across the course of their lives, sharing its savor—its moments, bitter and sweet."[6] He's right. That's because true friendships take time and effort. The trap is that we will stay in contact with so many 'friends' on Facebook that we end up ignoring the real friends and relationships that are in the same room with us. We can end up spending more time talking on the cell phone or chatting online than sitting down face to face to converse with those who are close by.

Real hands-on relationships are intentional about sitting across from each other and sharing life. In an age of cyber-relationships, the trap we may fall into is buying the lie that a large number of *virtual friendships* with sound-bite conversations and log-in/log-off connections are a suitable substitute for authentic friendships with real-time connections. In the world of relationships, sometimes less really is more.

## getting more out of less

Understanding the problem is only part of the process. Radical grandparents who take their Spring Keeper responsibilities seriously are committed to helping their grandchildren experience the real thing. Here are a few radical ways that courageous, intentional grandparents can make a difference and counter the virtual unreality game:

- Turn off all cell phones, iPods, and other electronic devices when you have guests in your home. I created a cell phone caddy I place by the front door when we are expecting family and guests. On it is a short poem I wrote asking our visitors to deposit their phones. It reads:

  *As family, friend or special guest,*
  *We want our time to be the best;*
  *So thank you for this one request*
  *To silence your phone and give it a rest!*

- Plan a special outing with your grandchildren ten years of age and older. This works well if you can take them one at a time, but a group outing works too. Plan it around an event or activity they would really enjoy, but no movies or electronic game arcades allowed. You might take them to a local museum, the zoo, a theme park, a theatrical play, plan a picnic or hike, go to the beach, or plan an excursion in the mountains. The possibilities are limited only by your imagination and physical abilities.

Whatever you do, one of the requirements must be that all cell phones or other electronic devices are left at home (you can keep one for emergencies). The objective is not only to have fun but to engage in meaningful conversation (which can be fun too). Parents may be included in the outing, but there is something special that happens when it's just you and your grandchild.

While spontaneity is good, you might want to think about some questions you would like to talk about when you are together. For example: *Who is your best friend? What do you most like about this friend? What do you think it means to be a friend? Besides TV or video games, what thing do you most enjoy doing? Why do you think God made you and put you here?*

Be sure to listen a lot. Encourage them to talk. It is very appropriate for you to share stories of your own life that might encourage them in some of the things they are trying to work through. When you do share your stories, don't dominate the conversation talking about you, and make sure you are transparent, honest, and relevant to the topic being discussed.

• Invite the grandkids to your house for a fun-filled tech-free adventure. Let them know ahead of time that they will not be using any modern technology devices like TV, computers, GameBoy, Wii, cell phones, iPods, iPads, microwaves, or radios. Explain that you are going to pretend you are pioneers. (If you know someone who owns a farm or ranch, this can be even more fun.) Create a whole day of activities that require you to work together and discover the wonders of life that can be experienced without tech-toys.

## trap #3: boredom syndrome

Boredom is another deceptive trap of technology. Boredom sprouts from the loss of contentment and quietude—the ability to be still and be at peace. It is the loss of wonder and imagination in life. A generation has grown up on our watch that is in constant need of amusement and external stimuli of some kind. Technology generates a constant source of 'noise' in our lives that drowns out any other voices or thoughts. This is a generation that is uncomfortable with silence and solitude. The ability to meditate and see the wonder in life is being sucked out of them by virtual substitutes.

One of the most common responses I hear from young people today when their technology toys have been taken away or restricted is, "I'm bored." When a kid says he is bored, what he is really saying is that he doesn't know how to be creative and inventive on his own. Kids who are easily bored are addicted to a variety of stimuli needed to hold their interest and keep functioning. Without all this extra stimuli, the only alternative is to be alone with one's thoughts. For most kids today that is a terrifying prospect. The ability to be still and think and create is the fruit of contentment, something media technology can rob if vigilance is not present.

A recent Kaiser Family Foundation study reveals that on average, kids between eight and eighteen are tethered to media-related devices the equivalent of nine hours a day.[7] That means that other than the time spent sleeping or in school, the rest of the time is spent on media devices like computers, TV, smart phones, video games, and often more than one at the same time. Even schools have given in to the tech obsession. Why? Because kids today struggle with creating imaginative activity without tech-toys to aid them. Smart phones have become the alternative solution to boredom for kids, and many adults.

The constant barrage of stimuli from media technology opens up a child's brain to be more "easily habituated" and less able to sustain attention according to the Kaiser study. In the long run, this means that it will be more difficult for this generation to stay focused, to complete tasks, or to defer gratification. Easily distracted, kids engrossed in various media are vulnerable to dangerous ideas and thoughtless decisions. This also means that young people obsessed with media technology will likely have trouble engaging with spiritual disciplines, faith, and truth.

The spiritual disciplines of prayer, meditation, fasting, and study are things that foster the development of our mind and our ability to relate to others. This is how our Creator intended for our brains to develop. Engaging too much of our time in the digital media world damages our ability to focus on what is true and excellent, and it makes it difficult to engage in spiritual disciplines that cultivate character and a relationship with our Creator.

Even the Parents Television Council (PTC) warns against too much media that can lead to a host of problems later in life, including intellectual development. "Even programming that is built as educational really has very little educational benefit for the youngster," according to Melissa Henson with PTC. "The child is more likely to grow intellectually and developmentally at a faster pace if they're not watching television and instead are looking at books…playing outside, or engaging with other kids or adults."[8] One high school student describes how he doesn't like to read books or novels because it takes too long. "You can get the whole story in six minutes online," he boasted. "I prefer the immediate gratification."

Clearly, Satan knows how to capture the hearts and minds of our youth through media technology. Technology is a dangerous trap when discernment and self-control is in short supply. A child's imagination and wonder of life can be robbed from them, producing a catharsis of the brain that does not know what to do without technological stimulants.

Is it possible to control technology in a way so that it does not rob the true delights and wonders of life from us? I think the answer is yes. Some of the suggestions made for Traps #1 and #2 can be helpful in building imagination and creative alternatives. The key is finding creative ways to engage your grandchildren in fun, stimulating activities that will replace the need to be constantly connected digitally. You'll also find some helpful resources in the Appendix.

Now, let's turn our attention to one more trap that needs to be addressed.

# trap #4: predator vulnerability

The truth about internet predators according to available statistics is scary. For example, Youth For Christ's *Enough Is Enough* internet safety program information claims that 77 percent of all predator contacts are with teens ages fourteen and older, mostly girls. Twelve percent of teenage girls admitted to eventually meeting strangers in person whom they first met while online. A majority (58 percent) of teens don't see anything wrong with posting personal information and photos of themselves on social networking sites.[9] The scary reality is that most teens knowingly chat with adult strangers online and seem unconcerned about it. Statistics like these are shocking, to say the least.

Technology does not police itself. It cannot prevent fraud, scams, or emotional terrorism on its own. Predators know how to use the internet and other technologies to prey on the numerous lonely and wounded hearts in our world. Emotional terrorism is the trademark of such predators. They know how desperately people want to feel loved and accepted. Children and teens, especially teenage girls, lacking an environment of love and blessing are particularly vulnerable.

Regardless of the controls you or your grandchildren's parents set up to protect them, if their lives are not being cultivated under the arbor of blessing and a loving home, they will be exceptionally vulnerable. No amount of controls can keep them from seeking love and acceptance somewhere if they are not getting it at home.

Older adults are targets as well. Many older adults avoid any use of the internet because they fear identity theft or becoming unsuspecting victims of deceptive emails and advertising. Older adults often find it difficult to grasp how someone could so cold-heartedly prey on trusting people without any conscience. We forget how wicked the heart of man really is.

Technology has made it possible for people to develop images and brand labels that create the illusion of being something they are not. Wicked men now have a palette of new tools for scamming innocent victims. The double-edged sword of technology offers both timesaving advantages along with the potential for devastating personal losses for you and your grandchildren. Vigilance cannot be short-changed.

The next chapter will explore more about applying due diligence in this area for the protection of our grandchildren.

# food for thought and discussion:

- Review the four different 'traps' mentioned in this chapter. What information is new for you or something you had not given much thought to prior to reading this section? How has this information changed your view of the dangers technology can present?

- Of these four 'traps' discussed, which present the greatest challenge for you or your grandchildren? Why?

- Which of the ideas or suggestions given seem most helpful to you? Which would be unlikely for you to use? Why?

# action step:

Review the action ideas presented in this chapter. Pick one or two ideas and develop a plan for how you intend to use them with your grandchildren and family. Ask someone you trust to pray with you as you do this then let that person know how it was received.

# due diligence

*"Wisdom is settling into our understanding without being too enamored by it."*
Shane Hipps

**E**ven though technology is not inherently evil, good tools in the hands of sinful men with evil intent serve as instruments of harm and destruction. Therefore, it is imperative that we understand not only the dangers technology poses but also how to apply vigilance and wisdom to thwart the potential risks and maximize the opportunities for good. Some basic due diligence and common sense will minimize or neutralize the downside of technology. I'd like to suggest a few due diligence procedures that can be applied to technology and life in general. These can aid us in constructing walls of protection for our families.

- **Affirm and bless frequently**:
  Every child needs constant affirmation of her worth and value as a person. This is especially important if your grandchildren are not experiencing a healthy home life. Divorce, parental abuse, and constant negative criticism set up a child for danger. Technology offers a diversion from the realities of life. When used to escape, good things rarely result.

  What kind of environment do your grandchildren find when they visit in your home? Do you affirm them or criticize them for the way they dress or style their hair? Hand-written notes and cards from time to time can provide very real, positive reinforcement of their value in your eyes. Tell them you are praying for them, and make sure you do it.

  Make a special effort to contact them when something exceptional occurs in their life. Perhaps they receive a school award or get a part in the school play. Let them know how proud you are. Don't forget to tell them so even on non-special occasions. Never allow Satan a foothold in their life by letting some stranger be the only source of acceptance and love they receive. (See Part Four for a more in-depth discussion of affirmation and blessing.)

- **Resist the "stuff monster"**:
  Don't give in to cultural pressures or the peer pressure your grandchild feels to always have the latest technology gadgets. Encourage their parents to do the same. You may not have much control over what your adult children allow, but you can keep your head about you in what you provide. Don't give in to the demands and pressures from

your grandchildren to buy them stuff they don't need or may lead to dangerous situations.

I know of a couple who took it upon themselves to buy their thirteen-year-old granddaughter a cell phone with an unlimited texting plan, even though the parents, who were divorced, had agreed not to give her a cell phone until she was sixteen. Unfortunately, neither parent was willing to be the 'bad guy' and take away the phone. She now spends most of her time texting her friends. Personal conversations have all but ceased around her family. The grandparents gave no thought as to whether she was ready to use it properly. They simply gave her what she wanted because they wanted her to like them.

- **Enter your grandchild's world**:
  Learn how to text and email (though email is largely passé now for teens and young adults). Find out all you can about social networking sites like Facebook, MySpace, Friendster, and Pinterest if that is what your grandchildren are doing. Talk to them about these things. Let them know you are interested in learning about some of these new technologies. Ask them to show you how it all works. Set up a Facebook account if you can, and communicate with them occasionally (disciplined discernment, remember?). Your presence on one or more of these sites will let them know you are in touch and aware of what is going on.

  If you do get involved in social networking, guard yourself. Don't let cyber-communication replace your personal, one-on-one communications. On the other hand, engaging with their world will communicate two things: 1) that you are interested in what they are doing and what they like; and 2) that someone is reading what they put on Facebook other than their peers.

  One teen told me she liked having her grandparents on Facebook because it helped her be accountable and responsible for what she wrote. It also gave her another means of communication with her grandmother, since she was long distant. She did make it clear that most kids don't want parents or grandparents jumping into every conversation and making embarrassing comments.

- **Cultivate an environment of nonthreatening dialogue**:
  Look for opportunities to discuss matters of morality, purity, and integrity with your grandchildren. Ask them how this impacts the way they use media technology. You might want to plan a special retreat or get-away with them to talk about these things.

Your role is not to protect them from all the evil in the world but to prepare them to make good choices with understanding and wisdom. Help them understand the consequences of greed, lust, pride, and immorality. Discussing these issues with an open, nonjudgmental spirit will encourage them to make good choices when no one else is there to help them.

- **Establish do-able boundaries**:
  Cell phones/smart phones, iPads, computers, TV, and video games should never be unrestricted and unmonitored. Allowing computers or cell phones in back bedrooms without monitoring procedures is dangerous and irresponsible. At the same time, you need to be reasonable without being foolish.

Here are some suggestions that you may find helpful in setting up appropriate boundaries in your own home:

- Be proactive: Help your grandchildren select the entertainment they watch. First, make sure that the options you have in your home are appropriate. Set time limits for watching TV or playing video games, and determine which TV programs, computer games, and video games are acceptable. Just because a video game is labeled E does not mean the content is appropriate. Make sure you know what the content is.

- As mentioned earlier, we have a no-cell-phone policy in our home when we have family or friends over for dinner or a special gathering. We ask everyone to silence or turn off their cell phones and deposit them in our cell phone caddy by our front door. By the way, we put our phones in the caddy too.

- Texting at the dinner table is unacceptable anytime. Do not answer the phone during meal times when family is gathered unless an important call is expected. That's the purpose for answering machines and voice mail.

- Sit down with your adult children and ask them what rules and guidelines they would like enforced for their children. Are there tech-toys they would prefer their children did not have? How might you help them manage and safeguard the technologies their children are allowed to have? Discuss some of the dangers and traps of technology.

You'll find recommended Technology Resources in the Appendix. Ask your adult children to review this list as well. Discuss the content and suggestions. Be proactive—don't wait till there is a crisis to address the subject.

- **Plan for a 'tech fast' occasionally**:
  I watched a talk show not long ago that followed a family that had been given the challenge to live without technology devices for twenty-four hours. Sounds like a great idea to me. I already suggested the tech fast idea in the previous chapter.

The important thing to remember is to make good use of the time with fun and meaningful relational experiences to replace the tech-toys. If you do it well, you may discover that your grandkids' tech-toys become less and less appealing, or at least less consuming of their lives. You'll find some ideas for tech-fast activities in the Appendix.

## maximize the good

Our closest friends, Bruce and Sally, are true long-distance grandparents. Their daughter, son-in-law, and two granddaughters live 'across the pond' in England. That means that they see each other only on those rare occasions when one or the other is able to gather the funds and make the crossing. Needless to say, that is not as often as they would like. Technology, however, offers a blessing they could not have imagined in 1997 when their first granddaughter was born.

Today, thanks to email, Facebook, and Skype, real-time, interactive visual communication is possible from anywhere in the world. Technology has allowed them to bridge the gap and ease the sting of not being able to hug their kids and grandkids. Now they can at least see each in real time and share part of their growth process, even though they are miles away. They can watch and listen as the girls play the piano, sing a song, or act out a skit. It's easier to keep current on special events or school activities going on at that moment. They can share thoughts or lessons that God is teaching them and new discoveries He is revealing each day. It may not be hands-on, but it's as close as you can get without actually being there. I'd say it is a major improvement over snail mail and expensive long-distance phone calls.

Long-distance grandparenting doesn't have to be quite so long distance these days if you are willing to learn about and take advantage of the new technologies that allow you to have instant, visual contact at little or no cost. There are so many other wonderful ways to use technology to share instant photos of fun times and special events, quickly gather information, plan a trip, and so much more.

It you don't know how to use Skype, FaceTime, or Google Hangout, I encourage you to seek out people who do and have them teach you. If you are unsure about how to use the internet safely and purposefully, ask a pastor or ministry leader in your church to offer a "Tech Workshop for Dummies" in your church.

Maximize the good opportunities that exist with technology today. Technology is a natural expression of the creative image of God in us. When we use it wisely and carefully, God's glory is magnified and we enjoy the fruit of His goodness.

But it's not enough to simply understand. We are called to rise up and respond to the call to rebuild what has been destroyed. Nehemiah could have rationalized it was too uncomfortable or too far away for him to do anything about the walls in Jerusalem. Yet he chose to trust God to do what no one else had been able to do. His unshakable belief in God's might and worth compelled him to take action. The rest of the story is history.

Our walls of protection founded in truth and authentic faith are in ruins. Who will rise up and follow Nehemiah's example to do something about it before it's too late?

# food for thought and discussion:

- What does affirming and blessing your grandchildren have to do with due diligence in technology?

- What are some ways you have chosen to enter your grandchildren's world without compromising your own values and standards? What are some new ways you could more intentionally enter their world and be an encouragement to them in the way they handle technology?

- How do you handle the establishment of boundaries in your home when it comes to cell phones, ipods, etc?  How important is it to discuss these things with your adult children? Have you done that? Why or why not?

- Read Proverbs 3:13-24. How will this change how you pray for your grandchildren? How you talk with them? How you look at the world around you?

# action step:

Read Appendix 1 on how to plan a *tech fast*. Set up a plan for doing one. Talk with someone about what you are going to do. Ask them to pray for you and then report to them how it went.

# p a r t   f o u r

# RISE UP!

*We kept at it, repairing and rebuilding the wall. The whole wall was soon joined together and halfway to its intended height because the people had a heart for the work.*

*When Sanballat, Tobiah, the Arabs, the Ammonites, and the Ashdodites heard that the repairs of the walls of Jerusalem were going well—that the breaks in the wall were being fixed—they were absolutely furious. The put their heads together and decided to fight against Jerusalem, and create as much trouble as they could. We countered with prayer to our God and set a round-the-clock guard against them…*

*The wall was finished on the twenty-fifth day of Elul. It had taken fifty-two days. When all our enemies heard the news and all the surrounding nations saw it, our enemies totally lost their nerve. They knew that God was behind this work.*

Excerpts from Nehemiah, chapters 4 & 6 (The Message)

# look out for the bricks!

g r a n d p a u s e :
*"Somewhere along the way we have missed what is radical about our faith and replaced it with what is comfortable...settling for a Christianity that revolves around catering to ourselves when the central message of Christianity is actually about abandoning ourselves."*

David Platt [excerpted from *RADICAL*]

**D**riving his brand-new Mercedes sports sedan through a downtown neighborhood, James drove a little faster than he should be driving through a residential area. He thought he saw something out of the corner of his eye to his right, but a quick scan of the line of parked cars revealed nothing out of the ordinary.

As he pressed on the accelerator he thought he saw a young boy between the parked cars. Just then he felt and heard a loud crunch as something smashed into the right front door of his new car. Slamming on his brakes, he shoved the car into reverse toward the spot where the collision occurred. James jumped out of his car and surveyed the damage. It was then he noticed a brick lying on the road. Someone had actually thrown a brick at his new car! He couldn't believe it!

Furiously James looked around for the culprit. He would give whoever threw that brick something to think about if he caught him. He spotted a young kid between the parked cars near the brick. "Are you the one who threw that brick?" he screamed as he lunged toward the boy. The boy looked terrified as tears streamed down his face.

Grabbing the boy by the shirt, James pushed him against the parked car and shouted, "What the heck do you think you are doing? You just smashed a brick into my brand-new car. I should smash your head with that brick. Do you have any idea how much it is going to cost to fix that? What were you thinking?"

Tears freely flowed down the boy's terrified face and onto the stranger's hands. "Please, mister...please! I'm so sorry about your car, but I didn't know what else to do."

Nodding toward another boy lying on the street between two cars, he continued. "I threw the brick because no one else would stop to help. My brother rolled off the curb in his wheelchair and fell. I can't lift him up."

Uncontrollable sobs now overtook the boy as he begged the driver, "Please help me get my brother back into his wheelchair. He's been hurt, and he's too heavy for me. Please, mister!"

James looked at the boy and then his brother lying the street. Overwhelmed by incredible shame for the way he reacted, James knelt next to the fallen boy and lifted him back into his wheelchair. Removing an expensive linen handkerchief from his suit coat, he knelt down and dabbed at the fresh cuts and scrapes on the boy's face. After a quick examination, he determined that he would be fine. Just a few bumps and scrapes was all.

"Thank you, mister, and may God bless you," the grateful boy said as he made sure his brother was secure in the wheelchair.

James silently watched as the young boy he had reamed out wheeled his brother away. Turning toward his new Mercedes, he looked at the dent in the side of the door. Tears now welled up in *his* eyes, but not because of the damage to his car. He decided right then that he would never fix that dent. He would leave it there as a reminder to never again go through life so fast that someone would have to throw a brick to get his attention.

Is it possible God is trying to get our attention today? The walls of our cities are in ruins. There are kids in our world—our own grandkids—who are desperately in need of someone to stop the mad rush long enough to help them find the hope and peace that can only come through the Gospel. He is calling us to stand up against the enemies of our time and not turn away from the rebuilding that needs to be done.

This nation watched as the Occupy Wall Street protestors took over city parks and public lands to speak out about their cause (whatever that was). It started with a few people who got the word out and who then mobilized thousands of people across the nation. Even with little more than an emotional appeal and an undefined cause, multitudes of people took to the streets and got the nation's attention.

Imagine what would happen if a few courageous grandparents and parents were as passionate about their cause to give hope to the next generations as the 'Occupiers.' Maybe there should be an Occupy Main Street rally across America calling for a return to the foundational principles of truth and freedom upon which this nation was founded. If a group of people without a defined cause can make an impact, why can't Christians make am even greater impact with a clear mission and cause for the good of all and the glory of God?

The wake-up call has been issued. Will we stop long enough to realize what is going on around us and take a courageous stand to do something about it? Or does someone need to throw a brick to get our attention? It's time for us to rise up, roll up our sleeves, and get a little radical.

## rad is cool

**Radical (adj):** *of or relating to root or origin; tending or disposed to make extreme changes in existing.views, habits, conditions, or institutions (Webster's Ninth New Collegiate Dictionary).*

Once popular among teens, the term *rad* is simply an abbreviation for the word *radical*. It is normally used as a superlative to express praise for something or someone who is 'cool' or 'awesome.' While not as popular in teen vernacular today as it once was, for our purposes it will help us tackle what it means to be a courageously *RAD* grandparent.

*RAD* grandparents are cool, not simply because they are fun, but because they embrace a bold view of their role and purpose as grandparents. They are eager and prepared to get up and go into battle for the territory of their grandchildren's hearts and minds…and to do so wholeheartedly.

For our purposes, *RAD* is an acronym for three characteristics that describe radically courageous grandparents who are not held back by what they cannot do. Rather, they are energized by what they can do. So, let's get to work and unpack these three *RAD* traits of courageous grandparents and see how we measure up.

## resolute

**My definition:** *Standing out from the crowd with an unshakable faith in God and His promises, unmoved by popular opinion, but wholeheartedly committed to God's purposes and glory.*

Sergeant Dakota Meyer received the U.S. Military's most prestigious award, the Medal of Honor, for heroics in Afghanistan in 2009. He was responsible for rescuing more than thirty comrades during a gun battle in Afghanistan, making five different trips into the teeth of enemy fire during a six-hour period to rescue wounded and fallen comrades. When asked about the risk he took doing what he did, Meyer, a corporal at the time, replied, "I didn't think I was going to die. I knew I was."

*RAD* grandparents are *resolute* about not letting fear or risk keep them from stepping outside their imagined 'safe places' to gain the better prize and rescue those they care about. Someone once said that consecration is resolve that is not afraid of sacrifice. Because RAD grandparents belong to Christ and follow Him wholeheartedly, they know life is never safe—in fact, it's downright dangerous. They also know that to play it safe involves far more danger and risk for everyone.

John Wilberforce did not change England's attitude toward the slave trade by playing it safe and surrendering to popular opinion at the time. Wilberforce was resolute and unshakable in his convictions about the appalling atrocities being done against human beings in the slave trade industry. He stood out from the crowd, not because of his great oratory, but because of his resolute persistence to do what was right regardless of prevailing public sentiment. His resolve radically changed his world, but not without a great deal of risk and personal cost.

If one man could make such a difference in his day, what might God do through the lives of millions of courageous, resolute grandparents standing upon an unshakable faith in God and the Gospel to live out the truth? That is the burden I have carried since that day I sensed the call of God in this cause. I want to challenge my generation—many who are now grandparents—to rise above the conventional view of grandparenting and passionately represent Christ to another generation. I never dreamed it would be this difficult to engage others in a cause that seems so obvious and pressing from my point of view, but I am compelled to press on.

I remain resolute in my determination to not give up on this cause because I know so much is at stake. I don't have all the answers, and I don't always do it right. I pray I may not be deterred from the task God has put before me. This book is born out of that resolve.

I'm grateful for the many grandparents I frequently meet or hear from who are equally resolved. Sadly, there are large numbers of grandparents claiming to be Christians who stand on the sidelines content to be 'good' grandparents.

Will you take your stand among the courageously resolute?

# audacious

**My definition:** *Embracing and enjoying life as God's workmanship with boldness, daring, verve, creativity and humility so that others may clearly see the greatness and splendor of God.*

I'm not big on bucket lists. They're okay, but they are usually more about the person creating the bucket list than anyone else. Don't get me wrong, there's nothing wrong with a wish list of things you want to do. There is a time and place for those kinds of dreams. The problem is that most bucket lists usually ignore the ultimate *how* question. How will the greatness and glory of God be displayed in what you want to do?

God created you as His workmanship for specific purposes, which He planned long before you were formed. These purposes, expressed as good works, truly give meaning to your life and produce the greatest delight. That being the case, it is *God's* bucket list that you and I should be pursuing with all the bold verve we can generate.

Do you have a bucket list? What's on your bucket list? Is it limited to the things *you* have always wanted to do but never had the chance, or does it express the things *God* wants you to experience but you're missing because you're too busy doing your thing?

In America the retirement deception greatly molds existing attitudes about bucket lists. We are told it is an honorable thing to pursue whatever you want because you've done your time and you deserve it. It takes some audacity to stand up against the prevailing winds of cultural nonsense and dare to do things differently.

Audacious grandparents are not afraid to think outside the box and make God look great in the way they live life. And they do it with humility, not arrogance, because they know they are God's workmanship. They understand that He is the Designer and Creator, and their purpose is wrapped up in His.

Audacious grandparents want to make history. The difference is that they understand it is still God's work, not theirs. So, while they can't create the future, they can choose to be an instrument of their Creator to create a future for their grandchildren that reflects His splendor. Evil men don't sit around and wait for permission to make the world what they want it to be. Your grandchildren cannot afford for you to sit around and hope someone else will step to the plate to do what you already know God expects of you.

There's a story that needs to be told—the true story about who we are, who God is, and what He has done. It's the Gospel, and it must not be diluted or reduced to little more than a fairy tale. The Gospel is the grand story of God's liberating and lavish grace to free us to experience Life (with a capital 'L') in Christ. It's a story worth telling well. Audacious grandparents never tire of telling it enthusiastically and creatively because they know something about the story. It is a powerful and wonderful story about the ordinary becoming something truly extraordinary.

Audacious grandparents are courageous. They know there is still much more living to do and adventures to experience before the silver cord is cut. They don't waste their time waiting for someone else to do what they have been called to do. Until the last breath is expelled, they live in the belief that they are still God's workmanship.

The race isn't over. We are not excused from the game to sit on the bench. Pastor and theologian Dietrich Bonhoeffer said, "A righteous man lives for the next generation." I'd say that demands a pretty audacious and courageous life!

## deliberate intentionality

**My definition:** *Confidently and obediently engaging with God's purposes to be a conduit of His extravagant grace, employing all He has given me to bless and compassionately represent Christ to another generation.*

Buck and Molly are courageous grandparents. They love their grandchildren—all eight of them. Like most good Christian grandparents, they talked about the Bible and their faith with their grandchildren. Even so they understood that the primary responsibility for spiritual training belonged to their adult children.

Early in their grandparenting experience, however, they realized that the role God had given them as grandparents was as vital a role for cultivating a legacy of faith in their grandchildren's lives as that of the parents. While their roles differed from the parents' roles, they recognized that their responsibility was essentially the same—to train up a child in the way he should go.

It didn't take long for them decide they needed to be more intentional about how they interacted with their grandchildren and passed on to them eternal truths about God, the world He created, and life's purpose. After discussing it with their own children and their spouses, they decided to implement a plan for a special event with the grandchildren that would hopefully encourage a hunger and thirst for God's Word. They also wanted to reinforce how much each grandchild is loved—loved by God, their parents, and their grandparents.

They decided it would be fun to host a family Grand Camp at their home in Colorado, which they called Felsennest, meaning "refuge on the rock" *(Matt. 7:24-25)*. A lot of planning and work went into making this effective and fun for the kids. The grandkids ranged in age from eight to fifteen and came from three different states. Everyone eagerly anticipated the week at Felsennest.

When they arrived they were each given t-shirts imprinted with the Felsennest logo, designed by Buck and Molly, and a verse paraphrased from Deuteronomy 26 that said, *"Celebrate all the good things God, your God, has given you and your family."* The entire week was filled with fun activities intentionally designed to reinforce Scripture learning and what it means to know and follow Christ wholeheartedly. Field trips, daily reward challenges, Scripture memory, fun games, exploring God's creation, theme dinners, and even chores were planned for each day.

The kids had a blast. In the process they learned much about life and God's purposes for them through the experience. Grandpa Buck and Grandma Molly had a good time too. In fact, they both felt they had experienced one of the true highlights of their lives. This was just the beginning of an ongoing adventure as intentional grandparents determined to live for the next generation as Christ's representatives.

So, maybe Grand Camp isn't your thing. Not all of us have the resources or abilities to do what Buck and Molly did. The point is that they stepped up to the plate and decided to do something intentional—something courageous and radical. They were not content to simply be fun grandparents. The impact they made on the grandkids happened because of their determination to step outside the usual expectations for grandparenting and deliberately embrace something much more intentional and purposeful for their grandchildren's sake.

Resolute, audacious, and deliberate—these are the things that characterize courageous grandparents. I know I'm not as *RAD* as I'd like to be. I have a lot of growing to do in each of these areas. Nevertheless, I am determined, like I hope you are, to be a truly *RAD* grandparent. Like Caleb of old, may my life be so wholeheartedly devoted to Christ that my grandchildren cannot help but know how great our God really is and want to know Him too.

# a page 32 perspective

One of the most convicting and life-challenging books I've read in recent times is John Piper's *Don't Waste Your Life.* Page 32 especially grabbed my attention and changed a great deal of my perspective of life as a follower of Christ. My understanding of why I am here and what my life ought to say to my grandkids was revolutionized. Here's what Piper wrote on page 32:

> "Life is wasted when we do not live for the glory of God. I mean *all* of life…We waste our lives when we do not pray and think and dream and plan and work toward magnifying God in all spheres of life. *God created us for this: to live our lives in a way that makes him look more like the greatness and the beauty and the infinite worth that he really is.* In the night sky of this world God appears to most people, if at all, like a pinprick of light in a heaven of darkness. But he created us and called us to make him look like what he really is. This is what it means to be created in the image of God. *We are meant to image forth in the world what he is really like.*"[1] (Italics mine)

Did you get that? We are created to show the world what God is really like—to *image forth in the world* His greatness, beauty, and infinite worth. That's what Nehemiah did as he rallied the people to finish the work in the face of opposition and ridicule. *"Remember the Lord who is great and awesome,"* he declared (See Neh. 4:14). Finishing the task in record time in spite of all the opposition, those under Nehemiah's command left no doubt about the greatness of God for those around them who witnessed this amazing feat.

Commenting on Jesus' startling proclamation that "whoever loses his life for my sake will find it," Piper again exhorts us to remember that it is "better to lose one's life than to waste it. If you live gladly to make others glad in God, your life will be hard, your risks will be high, **and your joy will be full.**"[2] And, I might add, the world will see the glory of God. Grasping this truth gives clarity to what it means to live as a *RAD* grandparent for the next generation.

Whether young or old, life is wasted when we try to be what we were never designed to be. God made you in His image and gave you a purpose as His workmanship. As we live out that purpose as a son or daughter, a wife or husband, a father or mother, an employer or employee, and a grandmother or grandfather, we make Him look great and display His glory for all to see. It's that simple. It is also diametrically opposed to the world's way of thinking. That's the beauty and joy of courageous living.

If our grandchildren, or anyone else for that matter, see in us a courageously resolute, audacious, and determined life that magnifies the greatness of God, then Christ is being lifted up. When that happens, in spite of our flaws, Jesus promises men will be drawn to Him. If they do not see the joy of a capital 'L' Life because of Christ in us, then we are wasting our life.

*RAD* grandparents are not focused on personal significance but God's greatness. If we waste life living for ourselves, we risk losing the opportunity to reveal to our children and grandchildren the true treasure of the Gospel for all eternity.

*RAD* grandparents understand that making God look great has a lot to do with the way we spend our assets for Kingdom purposes. Such men and women are legacy-builders, not barn-builders.

## drive off the lot

Imagine buying a brand-new car with a full tank of gas, getting into the car, and never driving it off the dealership parking lot. Day after day you come to the dealership, get in your new car, occasionally start the engine, but never put it in gear. You sit content to enjoy the new car smells and all the gadgets, but nothing else. It doesn't make any sense, does it? A car, after all, is designed to be *driven*, and last time I checked, that means starting the engine, putting it in gear, and driving off the lot.

As laughable as this illustration may seem, sadly it's the way many grandparents view grandparenting. Some decide it's too dangerous, too risky, or too much work at this time of life to get much involved. The best option is to simply avoid the hard work and let the parents take care of it.

It's easier to sit back in a more passive role, dodge some of the bullets, and do little beyond fiddling with the accessories—the fun stuff.

After all, at this stage of life, who wants to take on another major responsibility? Sure, it's fine to start the engine once in a while—you know, read a Bible story or pray at meals. But don't ask me to put it in gear and drive onto the highway of intentional, courageous grandparenting. It feels pretty comfortable just sitting in the parking lot.

If this describes you, you're missing out on the ride of your life! More importantly, your grandchildren are missing out. In fact, they're losing out.

*NOTE: If you'd like to know more about GrandCamp, where you don't have to do all the planning yourself, visit our web site at www.grandcamps.org.*

# food for thought and discussion:

- What would change in the way you live if the RAD qualities truly characterized your life? What are the obstacles to making these qualities a reality? Which of the three is most challenging for you? Why?

- Why do you think John Piper says that life is wasted when it does not give glory to God in all of life? Do you agree or disagree? Why? How do we "image forth" the greatness and beauty of God in our lives? In what ways are we guilty of doing just the opposite?

- What do you think your grandchildren would say about how you lived your life at your funeral?

# action steps:

List one practical way you can flesh out each of these three characteristics now:

a. Resolute:


b. Audacious:


c. Deliberate:

# live a legacy that outlives you

**g r a n d p a u s e :**
*"Those who give much without sacrifice are reckoned as having given little."*
Erwin Lutzer

The bumper sticker on the back of a large RV proclaims *I'm Spending My Kids' Inheritance!* The message may make us smile, but think about it. It's really nothing to smile about. Proverbs 13:22 says, *"A good man leaves an inheritance for his children's children."* The RV bumper sticker reflects a lack of understanding about the purpose of an inheritance. Maybe it's time to get some perspective.

Jim Stovall's, *The Ultimate Gift*, tells the story of Red Steven's plan to help his wild and irresponsible nephew, Jason, learn the truth about the true treasures of life. Jason's uncle had already died. He left his will in the capable hands of his best friend and attorney, Theodore Hamilton. As executor of the will, Theodore Hamilton makes sure Jason fulfills all the stipulations of the will, which include twelve tasks that must be completed exactly as instructed in order to receive his inheritance.

Jason is given no information about what the inheritance is—only that Red refers to it as the 'ultimate gift.' He reluctantly agrees to do what his uncle asked, hoping to receive a large financial windfall in return. What Jason didn't expect was how it would change him. Listen to what he says at the end of story…

> *"My Uncle Red's love for me in giving me the ultimate gift forever changed my life and who I am…and I am going to find a way to pass it on to deprived people who are as I was a year ago. I had no idea that the greatest gift anyone could be given is the awareness of all the gifts he or she already has. Now I know why God made me and put me on this earth. I understand the purpose for my life and how I can help other people find their purpose."*[1]

Jason was set free from his self-centered, entitlement world. He discovered a whole new way of living where the real value of a full life has little to do with material wealth. He learned it because his uncle chose to give him something that money could not buy. It was a gift that would free him from the bondage of self and things. Red knew that if he didn't do it, probably no one else would. Jason was worth too much to let him destroy himself and others.

I wonder how much we understand the things Red came to realize at the end of his life—that giving those we love more *things* does not build character or help them experience Life (with a capital '*L*'). The inheritance we pass to them can be a curse or a blessing. Our purpose is not to be a supply line for all the worldly pleasures our kids and grandkids desire. Rather, we are called to be a conduit of God's grace and blessing from which real pleasures abound. If what we truly treasure is the material estate we build, it is likely our descendants will consider that to be the only real value from our life as well.

Selfish living is wasted living. You are in a position to help your grandchildren discover a better way. To do so, you must be willing to invest the time and effort to show them. When they see you enjoying life with God as your source of delight and joy, they will be more likely to see God's glory and greatness as well. If your life displays Christ as the one passion you cherish above all, they will likely find themselves drawn to Him, and want the same for their life.

Of course, you can also choose to waste your life by selfishly spending what you have on yourself. If that's the choice you make, then the RV bumper sticker probably says it all. Not only will your life be a waste, but the investment opportunity of a lifetime will be lost as well. Is that the legacy you want to outlive you?

The greatest asset or gift you can give your grandchildren is you—your time, your values, your relationships, your faith and passion for Christ. A rich life displays the splendor and goodness of God. Piper claims that when our purest delight is showing others the beauty and joy of a life filled with a "passion for the supremacy of God in all things for the joy of all peoples," they will take notice. When they observe our confidence and enduring gladness even in the worst of times, they will want to know why.

Not only does a good man's inheritance display the glory and greatness of God, it reveals the high value he places upon his children and grandchildren. He does not give them gifts that have no value or that lead to harm. What are your grandchildren worth to you? Does the inheritance you are preparing for them reflect that worth?

That breathtaking moment when I held my first grandchild, I knew where I wanted to invest my life and resources. I had no idea what that would mean or where it would take me. Eventually it led to the founding of the Christian Grandparenting Network. My desire was to enlist and engage other grandparents who shared a passion for representing Christ to the next generations. Today I sense the urgency of the times even more. I am a Boomer grandparent. I want the grandparents of my generation to wisely invest all the resources entrusted to us for the next generation instead of throwing them away on useless things that ultimately disintegrate.

# purses with holes in them

I know that teaching from the Old Testament prophets is not a particularly popular thing to do these days. Yet, some of God's most important messages to His people, then and today, were spoken through these prophets. Consider, for example, the words of God through His prophet Haggai. He reprimands the people for putting so much effort and resources into building paneled houses for themselves while the house of God remained in shambles. *"Consider your ways,"* He warned. *"He who earns, earns wages to put into a purse with holes"* (Haggai 1:5-6 NASB). That sounds pretty much like our day.

Millions of today's grandparents spent enormous amounts of time and resources building their portfolios for themselves while their families and the nation lie in ruins. It's time to pay attention to God's warning about giving careful thought to our ways. Comforts and luxury rarely known at any other time in human history dominate our lives. Yet the pillars of truth and righteousness that give honor to our Creator and from which we receive His blessings lie crumbled around us. Our grandchildren are forced to navigate a sea of uncertainty and existential hopelessness with a leaky rowboat and no paddle or a compass to help them.

Branded as the 'me-generation,' baby boomers emerged and immediately stamped their imprint on the world. From Woodstock to Watergate to Wall Street, Boomers initially expressed themselves via love-fests, loud protests, and social activism. Before long they soon gave up their sit-ins for stock options and IPOs. We have devolved into a generation that lives by the philosophy of the foolish rich man of Luke 12—take life easy; eat, drink, and be merry.

Harry Gordon Selfridge founded what would become a chain of high-end department stores in the UK. The flagship store in London is second in size only to Harrod's. Known for his innovative and creative marketing style, Selfridge tirelessly led the charge to change the retail environment forever. His goal was to build a place where shopping would be a fun adventure and the customer was always right. He did just that and amassed a great fortune in the process.

Unfortunately, his addiction to the good life and fame did little to build a healthy home life. Then the Great Depression came and Selfridge lost almost everything. He had embraced the philosophy of life to eat, drink, and be merry with gusto and carelessness. He died in 1947 impoverished and alone. It's doubtful Selfridge ever thought about God's warning to Haggai to *consider your ways*.

Today there are no lack of fools who tell us that we should interpret the blessing of God in terms of things, pleasures, comforts, and safety. But beware—when that becomes our grid for evaluating God's blessing, we actually bring a curse rather than a blessing into our homes, our churches, and our businesses. We may not live the lavish life of a Harry Selfridge, but pleasure, beauty, wealth, power, and fame still often symbolize what we most cherish and value. Are we guilty of exchanging the truth of God for a lie? It seems the high price for the illusion we so foolishly embraced has now caught up with us.

Consider what we are reaping. The return we are now realizing on our investments should be obvious. Epidemic divorce and broken homes, narcissism, weak and spineless faith, miserly giving, and powerless community relationships are the products of our investments. Social, ethical, and moral responsibility has been sacrificed on the altar of folly and personal choice. It's time for us to admit that our sought-after wealth has been stashed in *purses with holes in them*.

We should not be shocked to see our own children and grandchildren seduced by this cursed delusion we helped birth. What is tolerated in one generation is deemed acceptable in the next, and finally fully embraced as normative in the third generation. Like the generations who came after Joshua's generation, we have chosen the path marked *Do-What-Is-Right-In-Our-Own-Eyes*.

It's time to take a good look at the world we helped make, ask God to search our hearts, repent for our foolishness, and then ask, "Lord, what would You have us do now?"

In the 1970s, theologian and author Francis Schaeffer asked a similar question, which we failed to take seriously enough. He asked *How Should We Then Live?*[1] It is a question we dare not ignore any longer. A good place to start addressing that question is to consider our ways. In other words, how are we using the assets God has given us?

Andrew Murray, South African pastor and writer in the early twentieth century, said this: "The world asks, 'What does a man own?' Christ asks, 'How does he use it?'" In case you haven't figured it out yet, there is a war going on. It is a spiritual battle for the hearts and souls of our grandchildren. What are we doing to make sure the assets we have been given are going to turn their hearts towards Christ and His righteousness?

The inheritance we leave for our children's children must accurately display the splendor of God's love and grace to show them that God is behind it all. How will we use what He has given us to invest for the future? However we answer that question, one thing is for certain: This is not the time for us to spend the kids' and grandkids' inheritance on ourselves!

Jim Elliott, martyred missionary to Ecuador, said it this way: "He is no fool who gives what he cannot keep to gain what he cannot lose." What does that look like in the context of who you are and what God has given to you? I'd like to suggest a new way of thinking about an old means of passing on an inheritance that might help you figure that out.

## not your ordinary will

Many Americans today have a living will. When you stop to think about it, it is a rather morbid document that authorizes someone we trust to carry out our wishes about the end of life. We are stipulating the conditions in which we would want to be *unplugged* from medical life support systems. Why we call this a *living* will is beyond me! We should just call it what it really is—a *death* will. After all, the purpose for it is to tell others how you want to die when certain circumstances occur.

I'd like to suggest a different approach to the idea of a *living will*. Instead of thinking of it in terms of a death will as we normally do, let's create a living will that is actually a *living* living will. All right, I recognize that deer-in-the-headlights look on your face. Stay with me. I'll try to make it clearer.

Imagine creating a Living Will (capital 'L', capital 'W') that has nothing at all to do with how we wish to be unplugged and allowed to die. Instead, this *will* describes how we wish to remain *plugged in* to God's purposes while alive and active. In other words, let's create a Living Will that describes how God wants us to invest our life assets for the next generations while we're still living.

This new *living* Living Will itemizes the assets God has given us. It then outlines how God wants us, as His trustees and *workmanship,* to invest those assets. It acknowledges that our assets are really God's assets. It further expresses our desire to invest them, dispose of them, or distribute them so that others will know the joy, the delight, and the great amazement of living life with a capital 'L' in Christ.

This simple, rewarding approach to the living will provides structure for living up to God's purposes for us. My father used to say, "Where there's a will, there's a way." I believe God has provided a way for us to reclaim the hearts and minds of our children and grandchildren for the Kingdom—if we have the will to do it.

Every human being on this planet has one life—and only one life—to live, invest, and spend wisely. When the funeral is over, our material possessions remain behind to be distributed to others, usually through a legal will or trust. We have no control over how those will be used. None of us will be around to oversee that process. It is possible that every material asset we leave behind will be wasted on worthless endeavors. The outcomes are out of our hands.

On the other hand, what would happen if millions of grandparents like us took a different approach to life? Imagine if we all used the pattern of Stovall's *The Ultimate Gift* to flesh out what it looks like to do the good works God prepared in advance for us to do. What if the ultimate gift we leave for the next generations is expressed through an ultimate *Living Will* that describes how we believe God wants both material and nonmaterial assets to be used for Kingdom purposes?

Notice I said material *and* nonmaterial assets. The traditional will only deals with material assets. This new Living Will paradigm is concerned with material as well as those unique nonmaterial assets we also possess. Often these have as much or more intrinsic value than any material asset in our estate. Nonmaterial assets include family, friendship, faith, knowledge, education, skills, talents, spiritual gifts, wisdom from life experiences, time, and so forth.

The point is that while both material and nonmaterial assets can be invested, spent, or disposed of while we're alive, only nonmaterial assets will be forever gone when we die and have failed to use them as they were intended. To unwisely hoard, hide, or carelessly waste these important assets, is to forever lose what was given for the purpose of blessing others. The reality is that we can't risk waiting. We must do it now, while we still have breath and the ability to do it.

A legal will may be useful for designating how your material things are to be distributed, but it is of no value for anything else. None of your nonmaterial, intangible assets can be distributed by anyone but you—in the flesh. Waiting till you die only guarantees two things. First, God's intended purpose for those personal endowments of your life will be diminished, if not lost entirely. You are the only one who can employ those assets with all the meaning and power for which they were intended in those relationships.

Second, failing to invest what God has given you means you miss out on the joyful privilege and rich reward of being God's special conduit of blessing for those around you. What incredible blessing might be missed if you do nothing? It's possible that God had in mind to supply something that only you can supply to someone in desperate need—perhaps in your own family. God delights in rewarding those who seek Him and obey Him. Why would you choose to lose the reward God wants to give by burying the gifts God has already given you to bless someone in a way no one else could do?

Moses spent forty years in the desert so God could prepare him for that ultimate purpose—to deliver the Israelites from the bondage of Egypt. And look at Caleb! At age eighty-five he understood that God had developed his physical strength and cunning so he could defeat his enemies and take the land God had earlier promised him. Why should you not believe that God has similar plans for you today? It's possible He has assembled and polished certain qualities and assets in you for a special purpose that has yet to be accomplished. Perhaps it has to do with your role as a grandparent. You have been called on stage for your biggest role yet.

There has been no other time in our nation's history when the children of our land are at such high risk as they are today. Do not minimize the danger or fail to seize the opportunity that you have *now*. God has cultivated your life so that you can put into play all you are and all you have to bless and equip these *little ones* for these turbulent times.

This is the *Living* Living Will Principle. It is a simple, yet potent, tool for expressing and displaying the *glory* of your life created in Christ Jesus. It takes courage and faith to embrace all that God has prepared for you as His workmanship. Courageous grandparents live to be a conduit of blessing for another generation. The *Living* Living Will is a tool to help you do exactly that.

# food for thought and discussion:

- Why is selfish living wasted living? How does the image of 'purses with holes in it' impact your understanding of wasted living?

- What does it mean to 'consider your ways'? How can the concept of a new Living Will paradigm assist in this process?

- Have you ever thought about the non-material assets you have? Why would these be important to consider in this new Living Will approach?

# action step:

Ask God to show you how your use of the assets He has given you in your life matches up with His purposes. Take the step of 'considering your ways' by asking Him to reveal whether the way you spend your life makes Him look great or you

# plugged in or plugged up?

**g r a n d p a u s e :**
*"When it comes time to die, make sure that all you have to do is die."*
Jim Elliott

The process involved in building your personal Living-Living Will is rather simple. It is not easy, however. In fact, plugged-in living according to God's agenda is a dangerous process. Some prefer to play it safe, and in doing so, end up plugging up the conduit that allows God's blessings to be poured out through you. The truth is that it is dangerous to be a follower of Jesus Christ. It's the cost of following Christ, and we do it because of the joy set before us. The world will not understand, and the enemy will resist. Like Nehemiah, it will require a wholehearted commitment to each step in the process to achieve the results God wants to achieve.

Are you prepared to count the cost to live as a conduit of God's blessing for the next generations? If so, here are some basic steps required to stay plugged in to God's purposes for you and all He has given you. They are the means for building a *Living* Living Will so that your life will make God look great and glorious:

**Step 1:** Inventory the contents of your asset portfolio—material and nonmaterial;

**Step 2:** Inquire of the Lord concerning His plan for using those assets; and

**Step 3:** Establish an action plan for distributing or investing those assets accordingly.

That's not too complicated, is it? It does require some resolve, wisdom, and faith like Nehemiah in order to build this *Living* Living Will legacy. Armed with God's Word and divine power, you have all you need. So, let's move on.

The disposition or spending of both material and nonmaterial assets must be wisely utilized so they fulfill God's purposes for the person or persons to whom they will be dispensed. When dealing with material assets, we want to consider how we can *reasonably* provide for our children and grandchildren. Just remember that it does them no good to give them all the materials things they could want, and in so doing "rob them of everything that makes life wonderful," as Red Stevens learned late in life in *The Ultimate Gift*. The lessons of hard work, responsibility, and diligence are not learned through handouts.

John Wesley was a man of significant wealth in his day, but he spent little of it on himself. His charity was limited only by his means. He gained his wealth from the hymns he wrote and the books he penned. At one period in his life it is reported that he gave away forty thousand pounds of sterling—a fortune in his time. Yet, when John Wesley died, his estate was worth twenty-eight pounds. He died poor, at least, as the world judges poverty. John Wesley would argue that he died the richest man on earth. I think God would agree.

Whether we have much or little, the attitude we have towards material possessions tells everyone we know what we truly treasure. Jesus said, *"Where your treasure is, there will your heart be also"* (Matt. 6:21). He exhorted us to store up our treasures in Heaven, not on earth where they rust and decay. Author Randy Alcorn calls this the Treasure Principle. In his book by the same title, he reminds us that each of us is storing treasure either in heaven or on earth. There is, however, only one good place to store them…

> By telling us to store up treasures for ourselves in heaven, [Jesus] gives us a breathtaking corollary, which I call the Treasure Principle: **You can't take it with you—but you can send it on ahead.**
>
> It's that simple. And if it doesn't take your breath away, you're not understanding it! Anything we try to hang on to here will be lost. But anything we put into God's hands will be ours for eternity… If we give instead of keep, if we invest in the eternal instead of in the temporal, we store up treasures in heaven that will never stop paying dividends. Whatever treasures we store up on earth will be left behind when we leave. Whatever treasures we store up in heaven will be waiting for us when we arrive…
>
> The money (and other valuable assets) God entrusts to us here on earth is eternal investment capital. Every day is an opportunity to buy more shares in His kingdom.
>
> You can't take it with you, but you can send it ahead. It's a revolutionary concept. If you embrace it, I guarantee it will change your life.[1]

Do you know what you have in your possession to 'send ahead'? It's time to take inventory.

# step 1:
## *make a list—check it twice*

The first step for creating your own *Living* Living Will is to know what you have to pass on or invest. Some things may not be immediately apparent. Don't overlook the seemingly minor things in your life like knitting, whittling, or gardening. By all means, tap into those unique, well-cultivated abilities that stand out in your life. They are all gifts from God intended for you to share with others.

That's what Rita did. Rita is an artist and grandmother. Soon after her grandchildren were born she began investing in them through her love for art. It wasn't long before she recognized a natural passion and ability for art in her granddaughter, Sofia. Rita eagerly seized the opportunity to nourish and encourage those artistic abilities through her own assets as an artist. She made sure Sofia always had ready access to Grandma's art supplies and her time.

Rita spends many hours helping Sofia develop her natural skills. She began by helping Sofia discover the creative work God had placed inside her that was unique to her, even at five years of age. As they paint together, Rita uses those moments to weave God's truth into Sofia's life so that she will understand how her art expresses the glory of God and serves as an act of worship of her Creator.

At age four, Sofia was invited to participate with her grandmother in their church's Christmas Eve services. Together they painted a Christmas scene as the congregation sang "Angels We Have Heard on High"–and they did it at six consecutive Christmas Eve services in a single day! That sounds like a lot for any adult to handle, let alone a four-year-old. Interestingly, Rita noticed that Sofia seemed more energized with each successive service.

"We underestimate what children can do for the Kingdom," Rita said. "I wanted to give her an opportunity to express this talent God had given her as an act of worship. Our art has been a common thread that has bonded us together and drawn us close. My job is not to conform her to my expectations or her parents' expectations for her life. I am there to help her find the freedom to become the person God created her to be in His image. I have been amazed to see the growth in her abilities and her understanding of God's truth in just the last year since we did the Christmas Eve services together."

# unpack your portfolio

As you unpack your personal portfolio of material and nonmaterial assets, think of them as *advantages* or *resources* that uniquely express who you are. You are God's masterpiece, created in His image. You are the canvas upon which the brush strokes of your life are painted, revealing His beauty and splendor expressed in the glory He has given you through the talents and assets you received. There's no reason to try to imitate someone else or imagine that you have nothing special to offer. You are uniquely created to be a conduit of blessing for those around you that no one else can be. Extraordinary artistic abilities like Rita's are not required to powerfully impact your grandchildren. Who you are is extraordinary because you were made in God's image. Never underestimate the significance of what you do have.

Age or physical capacity must also not be allowed to detract you from what you have to offer. You are a pipe, a conduit, through which God desires to lavishly pour out a rich bounty of gifts, talents, skills, time, experiences, knowledge, and wisdom for the blessing of another. This is all part of His amazing grace! Remember, you are His workmanship. He doesn't hand out inferior, worthless gifts. Your job is to open your hand to release what He has given you. If you clench your fist and hold back, you only serve to plug up the pipe.

As you build your list, you may discover some things that may be used only once, or perhaps a very limited number of times. Others will be used over and over again to bless the same person or many different individuals. How or how much they are used is irrelevant. The objective is to honestly acknowledge all that God has given you. Identifying the gifts you have is not boasting. It is giving glory to God for His goodness and grace in your life as His image-bearer. Your glory is His glory.

Material assets are fairly easy to identify. The intangible, nonmaterial assets may require a little more thought and investigation. You may not be used to thinking about some things as assets. Just jump in and ask God to show you what you need to know. Until you start the process, you may not realize how many assets you actually possess.

As you're making your list of nonmaterial assets be sure to include things like creative gifts and talents (art, writing, music, engineering, technology, carpentry, sewing, baking, etc.), love for reading, storytelling, knowledge (science, history, mathematics, Bible, etc), humor, hospitality, spiritual gifts, gardening, athletics, and important relationships. You will undoubtedly think of other things. And don't ignore those less-obvious assets. If you have an outstanding artistic ability like Rita's, don't lose sight of the other assets you possess that may be equally important for blessing someone.

For example, in the story of *The Ultimate Gift*, Red Steven's friendships were among his most powerful assets. They became the means through which he was able to achieve his objectives with his nephew. Your friendships and family relationships along with all of your life experiences are advantages you have to help another generation awaken to the wonders of God's purposes for them.

As you list your material assets, don't limit them to money, stocks, houses, and jewelry. Some of the most valuable material assets you have may hold very little monetary value. Memorable heirlooms, tools, recipes, books, letters, or journals are examples of material assets that can be especially meaningful when lovingly and intentional presented. Use the Asset Portfolio form in the Appendix to help you unpack your personal assets.

Remember two things as you work through this process. First, this is not a way to boost your ego by calling attention to the wonderful person you are and spotlighting certain notable assets. This isn't the time to contact the local TV station to do a story about your generosity. This is about making the Lord look great, not you. We all like to receive strokes from others; that's natural. But pride is sin and will hinder your ability to be God's channel of blessing in the lives of those He wants you to touch. These are not *your* assets—they are His, entrusted to you for His purposes. There is nothing wrong with receiving affirmation of the gifts and assets God has given to you. Such affirmation can be very helpful. However, guard your heart against pride, which God opposes.

Second, don't think of this as a bucket list. In other words, this is not an attempt to put together a list of things *you* always wanted to do before you kick the bucket. This is simply an inventory of what God has given you to invest or spend for someone else according to His purposes for your life and theirs. If you maintain the right perspective, you will discover how fun and exciting this adventure is and how much it fulfills your deepest desires more than any selfish bucket list could do.

Remember that humility is more than *not* thinking too highly of yourself— it is also being careful not to underestimate who you are and what God has supplied to you. You can make excuses why you can't do this, but the truth is there are no excuses, only possibilities. The possibilities are restricted only by your view of God and life, and whom God has made you to be. So, celebrate what you have been given!

Now that you know what you have been given, what do you do with it?

## step 2:
### *drill down—look up*

You're off to a good start. You've made a list. The next step is to lay aside any notions about what *you* want to do with them. Before you go any further, get on your knees and ask God what *He* wants to do with what He gave you.

Drill down to the important lessons and truths associated with each asset that are essential to pass on. How well you drill down is directly related to how much you look up and submit to the One who gave you what you have. Only by surrendering your agenda to God's will are you in a position to understand what these are about and who is to be blessed.

In Luke 12, the rich man in Jesus' parable exposed the true condition of his heart as he surveyed all the wealth he had accumulated. "He thought to **himself**, 'What shall **I** do? I have no place to store **my** crops.' Then he said, 'This is what **I'll** do...'"

Let's be honest—this was a man most of us would envy today. Here was a man who, through hard work and careful planning, achieved great success. Jesus wasn't condemning the rich or the accumulation of personal prosperity. He was pointing out the foolishness of those who continue to prosper but forget where their wealth comes from—and what it's for.

This man contracted spiritual amnesia by allowing greed to capture his heart and cloud his perspective about true riches. He foolishly replaced the imperishable riches of God with the perishable and foolish temptations fueled by greed. His energy was focused on building more barns rather than building a legacy of eternal riches that made God look great.

Compare his attitude to that of Nehemiah who stood up against those exploiting the poor and defenseless in his day. Nehemiah chose not to take advantage of all the privileges he had as governor in Judah. Instead of hoarding the best for himself, he fed scores of people at his table and refused to place heavy demands on the people for his own personal gain. For Nehemiah, wealth was a means of blessing others and magnifying his Creator—not for building his own estate.

In simplistic terms, there are two types of people in the world—those who live solely for what they can accrue for themselves, and those who see themselves as pipes or conduits through which *what they have* and *who they are* combine for the purpose of serving others. One is a temporal perspective. The other is eternal.

Once again, John Piper nails it on the head:

> The greatest joy in God comes from giving his gifts away, not in hoarding them for ourselves. It is good to work and have. It is better to work and have in order to give. God's glory shines more brightly when he satisfies us in times of loss than when he provides for us in times of plenty.... The world is not impressed when Christians get rich and say thanks to God. They are impressed when God is so satisfying that we give our riches away for Christ's sake and count it gain.[2]

Legacy is not merely about what we leave behind after we die. It is our spiritual DNA that directs how we live out our lives now. It is not just what we do, but what we do because of who we are in Christ. We are born of imperishable seed as new creatures with renewed minds and hearts. New creatures live differently. That legacy will be remembered long after we have been forgotten.

Many of the children, youth, and adults we will bless through the assets God has placed in our care are looking in vain in the wrong places for some sense of meaning and value. Giving them more *things* does not help them find what they are looking for. This is about investing all that makes up our lives in Christ. It is investing so others can discover and experience the ultimate goodness of God. This is how lives are transformed, blessings are unleashed, and treasures are stored up in Heaven. It's the *Living* Living Will Principle.

# step 3:
## *from the what to the who*

Several years ago a story appeared in a popular magazine about a couple that retired in their early fifties. They decided to spend the rest of their lives wandering the beaches of Florida and other parts of the world. Their objective for their retirement years: to collect shells. This was not a scientific journey. It was just how they wanted to spend their time. Upon learning about this story, my first reaction was, "You've got to be kidding! Why would someone want to spend their latter years roaming the world looking for seashells?"

What are you doing with the opportunities God is giving you? Do you know what you would say to the Omnipotent Creator of the Universe, the King of kings and just Judge of all men, the One who gave Himself so we could have eternal life, if He asked you this question: "Tell me, [insert your name], what did you do with all the assets I gave you to invest for My Kingdom and My glory?" Can you imagine standing before your Creator and having to answer that question by confessing, "Well, Lord, I gathered seashells, or I played golf, or I did nothing?"

You may not be spending your life collecting seashells, but is it being spent on things and activities that are just as useless? Perhaps an honest answer to that question may not align with what the Bible says God's intent is for us as His workmanship. It's never too late to change that, however.

The Lord has promised a liberal dose of wisdom to those who ask. This is a good time to ask. You will need such wisdom for this final step—to create another list. This time you will be creating a list of the people in your life God is directing you to bless through your assets. Write down their names, and then begin to ask God to show you how to match up your various assets with the people on your list. (See the Living Will Worksheet in the Appendix.)

Pray over each person on your list one at a time, asking God to reveal how to best use that asset to bless that person or persons, and show them God's goodness. Write down what you believe God wants you to do. Some tasks will be very simple and easy to do. Others may require a little more planning and work. Whatever you do, don't over-think the process and make it too complicated. You want to be authentic and focused on how to bless that person, not make him or her like you.

I encourage you to make use of the 14-Day Living Will Prayer Guide in the Appendix as a tool to help you maintain a pliable heart before God. Allow Him to fill you with His wisdom and understanding in this process. God bless you as you plunge into the incredible opportunity before you! Let me pray for you as you begin…

*Our Father, who made the heavens and the earth and all that is in them, and then made us in Your image, we kneel before Your throne in gratitude for the mercy and grace that You lavished upon us by the sacrifice of Your Son. It is under that Atonement, the righteousness of Christ, that we come before You and surrender our lives and passions to You for the purposes for which You made us from the beginning.*

*We are Your workmanship—we are not self-made men and women, masters of our souls. You are our Master and the Giver of Life. You have made us in Your image that we might display Your glory and splendor for all to see throughout all generations.*

*Now we ask, in view of Your tender mercy and great goodness, show the grandparents reading this how to use what You have placed in their hands so they might faithfully live and leave a true Living Will for the next generations—a living legacy of Your love and grace. As grandparents and parents, we desire to bless our children and grandchildren through these assets You have given us.*
*We want them to know Your greatness; we long for them to understand Your mighty power and Your wondrous grace. We yearn for that day when they will put their trust in You and follow You with all their hearts. We wish for them the life You meant for them to live according to Your perfect plan. Keep us humble, Lord, patient, kind, and forgiving that may they see Jesus in us.*

*In Your holy and precious Name, the Name of Jesus, I pray. Amen.*

Along with the wondrous assets God has given you for His purposes, He also calls you to be the voice of blessing for your family. Walk with me now through the process of restoring the power of the spoken blessing in your family.

# food for thought and discussion:

Read Matthew 25:14-30

- What do you think the 'talents' of this passage represent for us today? Have you ever stopped to evaluate what your assets are?

- How do you think the Master would respond to you if He returned today and demanded an accounting of how you have used the assets He entrusted to your care?

- If you were to ask your grandchildren what they think is most important in your life based upon how you use all the assets God has given to you, what do you think they would say? What would your neighbors say?

- We often think of "assets" in monetary or material terms. What are the nonmaterial assets God has also given us that demand equal attention and stewardship?

# action steps:

- Make an inventory of all of your material and nonmaterial assets this week.

- Ask God to show you how He wants you to use them to bless your children, your grandchildren, and others in your life.

- Discuss ways the group could celebrate the implementation of a Living-Living Will ceremony as a way of teaching the next generations the purpose of all God has given to us.

- Consider watching the film, *The Ultimate Gift*, together at some designated time, perhaps as a social event. Invite children and grandchildren to watch it with you and discuss.

p a r t   f i v e

# BUILD UP!

*By the seventh month the people of Israel were all settled in their towns. On the first day of that month they all assembled in Jerusalem, in the square just inside the Water Gate. They asked Ezra, the priest and scholar of the Law, which the Lord had given Israel through Moses, to get the book of the Law. So Ezra brought it to the place where the people had gathered—men, women, and the children who were old enough to understand. There in the square by the gate, Ezra read the Law to them from dawn until noon, and they all listened attentively.*

*As soon as he opened the book, they all stood up. Ezra said, "Praise the Lord, the great God!" All the people raised their arms in the air and answered, "Amen! Amen!" They knelt in worship, with their faces to the ground. Then they rose and stood in their places, and the…Levites explained the Law to them…They gave an oral translation of God's Law and explained it so that the people could understand it.*

*When the people heard what the Law required, they were so moved that they began to cry. Nehemiah, who was the governor; Ezra, the priest and scholar of the Law; and the Levites who were explaining the Law, told all the people, "This day is holy to the Lord your God, so you are not to mourn or cry. Now go home and have a feast. Share your food and wine with those who don't have enough. Today is holy to our Lord, so don't be sad. The joy that the Lord gives you will make you strong."*

Excerpts from Nehemiah, Chapter 8—Good News Translation

**The Lord spoke to Moses, "Tell Aaron and his sons, 'This is how you are to bless the Israelites. Say to them:**
*"The Lord bless you and keep you;*
*The Lord make his face shine upon you,*
*And be gracious to you;*
*The Lord turn his face toward you,*
*And give you peace." (Italics mine)*
**So they will put my name on the Israelites, and I will bless them.'"**
*(Numbers 6:22-27)*

# unleash the power of blessing

**g r a n d p a u s e :**

*"God does not do anything with us, only through us."*

Oswald Chambers

"**W**e decided to jump in with both feet!" Steve remarked after he and his wife returned from a blessing workshop I taught in Minneapolis. They decided to implement the principles they learned about the spoken blessing in their own family. Thanksgiving Day was just around the corner. The whole family would be gathered. It would be the perfect time to put their plan to work.

"We prayed each day leading up to our Thanksgiving gathering and made a list of all the special attributes and characteristics we had observed in each of our children and grandchildren. We prayed that the Holy Spirit would provide the right timing and location for this special occasion. And He did!"

Steve's big weekend arrived, and everyone was there. Following the traditional Thanksgiving feast, everyone spilled into the yard for another family tradition—a flag football game. Both participants and spectators had a great time in spite of the chilly Minnesota temperatures. Soon, cold and tired bodies gave in to a welcome time around the campfire to relax and warm up with some hot chocolate.

"The setting was perfect!" Steve recalled. "We shared with everyone how proud and fortunate we were to have a family like ours. With football fresh in their minds, we asked for responses to the question, 'How is family like a football team'? To our amazement everyone jumped into the discussion. Even the three-year-old shared ideas about helping and loving each other. Others shared about the different roles we each play and the importance of encouraging each other and working as a team. We could not have scripted a better introduction to the time of personal blessing.

"One by one, each child came and sat on our laps. We spoke to each of them about a special God-given talent or characteristic we saw in them. The children listened intently—more intently than at any other time we could remember with our grandchildren. Something transformational was taking place in that moment. God's presence was among us and was felt by all. Even our ten-year-old grandson asked if we could do this again."

For generations the Hebrew community has used the spoken blessing on a regular basis as an integral component of family life. Even today, many traditional Jewish families speak blessings over their children during Sabbath observances. A beautiful picture of this practice is played out in the movie, *Fiddler on the Roof.* The scene shows the family gathering for the Sabbath meal in which the parents, Tevye and Golde, sing a stirring song called "Sabbath Prayer." The words meaningfully express the substance of the traditional Jewish blessing. Here's a sample:

> *May the Lord protect and defend you. May He always shield you from shame.*
> *May you come to be in Israel a shining name…*
> *Favor them, Oh Lord, with happiness and peace. Oh, hear our Sabbath prayer. Amen.*
> (Lyrics written by Jerry Bock and Sheldon Harnick)

The practice of spoken blessing has been around since the very beginning of human history. It's not just an interesting storyline for a movie scene. God's first act after creating man and woman was to bless them. Genesis 1:29 says, *"And God blessed them, and God said unto them, 'Be fruitful and multiply, and fill the earth, and subdue it; and have dominion over the fish of the sea, and over he fowl of the air, and over every living creature that moves upon the earth.'"*

From the beginning, God set the example for earthly fathers and mothers to speak blessing into the lives of the next generations. Restoring this ancient practice could save an entire generation of young men and women from destruction decisions.

## more than words

Somewhere along the way the practice of spoken blessing has been largely abandoned. Most Christian families have never given it any thought. I don't recall hearing a pastor preach on the subject. This lack of teaching may explain why it is not often practiced in the Christian community today. Grandparents are in a unique position to create a tradition that should be part of every family. It is a role we should be modeling and teaching to the next generations for their sake.

The effectiveness of the spoken blessing rests on the condition that it is more than a rote recitation of empty religious words. Traditions devoid of meaning, purpose, and compassion produce no more effect than a fine mist sprayed into a hot, dry wind.

On the other hand, intentional, authentic words of blessing spoken into a child's life are like a cool drink of water refreshing a parched throat.

To *bless* literally means to "speak well of another." When the recipient of blessing knows how deeply we love and care about him or her, the impact can be transformational, even when the same words are used over and over.

When I asked my wife to marry me, I told her then that I loved her. Suppose I said to her, "Look, I told you when I asked you to marry me that I loved you. That should be enough. I don't need to keep saying it." Do you think she would be impressed? I'd probably be sleeping in the garage at night. No one tires of hearing "I love you" from someone who means it. The frequent repetition of that simple phrase has amazing power to keep a relationship fresh and strong. In the same way, no child ever tires of hearing words of blessing when spoken with love and sincerity.

Co-authors Gary Smalley and John Trent wrote many years ago about the importance of speaking blessing for families in a book entitled *The Blessing*. In it they describe the biblical elements found in a meaningful family blessing:

"A family blessing begins with <u>meaningful touching</u>. It continues with a <u>spoken message</u> of high value, a message that pictures a special future for the individual being blessed, and one that is based on an <u>active commitment</u> to see the blessing come to pass." [1]

Written in 1986, this book should have awakened parents to a desperately needed and obviously missing component of communicating God's love to our children. Somehow the message was missed or ignored. I wonder how much different the family picture would be today had we paid attention and heeded the call to restore the biblical practice of blessing in our families back then. I pray we are not too late.

The authors outline five elements of blessing in their book. I have condensed those five into three elements, which I believe adequately encapsulate the essence of the spoken blessing. God has not dumped a complicated process in our lap for blessing others. Anyone who chooses can do it. My hope is that you will grasp the value and importance of implementing the family blessing. Imagine the impact upon our families if thousands of grandparents across this land began practicing this good work in their families.

I have been teaching the principle of spoken blessing at our GrandCamps, conferences, and workshops for more than a decade now. It is a powerful means of communicating God's purpose and high value to each person involved. Remember, however, that the purpose of blessing is not to build your grandchildren's self-esteem so they can feel good about themselves. The purpose of speaking blessing is to serve as a conduit through which God's grace can flow so they understand who they are and how precious they are. The blessing becomes a means for providing a regular, tangible encounter with the transformational power of God. We confirm His gift of grace and His favor through the laying on of hands and speaking truth into another's life. Our goal is that those receiving the blessing may know Jesus Christ as their Lord and Savior and choose to wholeheartedly follow Him always.

The spoken blessing incorporates three critical elements that unleash the power of God's grace in an individual's life. They are:

1. A SPOKEN MESSAGE of *high value* and a *special future*;

2. MEANINGFUL TOUCH; and

3. AN ACTIVE COMMITMENT to personally support the one being blessed.

# element #1: say it

We're all familiar with the children's verse, "Sticks and stones my break my bones, but words can never hurt me." The truth is that this verse sends the wrong message. We know that words are powerful weapons that can be used either to bless or curse even the most thick-skinned. Some do handle it better than others, but most of us have a difficult time handling verbal abuse. The words of someone in authority can be unusually powerful for good or evil in a person's life, especially a child.

Do you remember the story of Howard Hendricks? His life changed direction partly because a teacher chose to engage with him as a conduit of God's blessing rather than continue the curse others had already pronounced upon his life. His teacher, Miss Noe, was determined to speak blessing into a young boy's life so that a cursed life could be transform into a blessed life by the grace of God.

There is a desperate need today for older adults who will engage with younger generations and communicate blessing in their lives. They need to know that God cherishes them and has already planned in advance a special future for them. They need to know someone believes in them and will stand with them on the journey. Your grandchildren are among them.

You are in a unique position to speak life-giving blessings into the lives of your grandchildren as no one else can. You can overpower the flood of curses flowing into their lives by flinging open the floodgates of divine blessing upon them. The key is authenticity.

Children and youth know when someone genuinely cares about them. Only when they know you care will they be able to receive the words you speak. Therein lies power of the spoken blessing. But speak it we must. The words "I love you" stir the heart with a powerful reminder of what is true. The words "May the Lord bless you…" carry the same power.

Spoken blessing is not reserved for the gifted or the well-behaved child any more than genuine love is limited for those who are compliant and easy to love. Every man, woman, and child needs to hear words of blessing by those with significant influence in their lives.

## what we say

The substance of the words we speak is vital. Specific words of blessing spoken from a loving heart speak life and hope into the life of a child or adult. The biblical examples for speaking blessing entail two critical truth messages: The first is an affirmation of a person's *high value*. The second involves picturing *a special future*. These two messages convey the truth that every person on this planet is made in the image of God and created with purpose. This is the glory of man over every other living creature in God's creation. Without an understanding of these two foundational truths, life is devoid of hope and meaning.

High value is not the same thing as self-esteem. Self-esteem is exactly that—esteem determined by what *we* think of ourselves. The source of true esteem is not found in self but in our Creator. It is the esteem of God that gives us our high value.

When we speak blessing to our child or grandchild, we are affirming that which God has already declared to be true. They are valued because their Creator made them in His image, not because they perform in a certain way. He loves them with an everlasting love and proved it at Calvary. We are proclaiming the glorious truth of the Gospel. It is grace alone, not personal merit, which saves them from the lies they have embraced.

Blessing softens a rebellious heart with a touch of the Father's heart. It reminds them that their deepest desires are satisfied in Him alone. God sent His only Son as proof of the high value He places on each person. Among all of God's creation, only man is privileged to receive the highest value stamp of the Creator.

Do not minimize the importance of the high value we convey to our children or grandchildren when we speak blessing to them. The affirmation of our words confirming our love for them because of who they are, not what they do, is huge. They need to know that we cherish them more than our own life. It is not foolishly making them the center of the universe so that they imagine that all other life revolves around them. That is narcissism. Our goal is to communicate that nothing can change our love or God's love for them.

Related to high value is the picturing of a special future. The special future we picture affirms the work God is doing and has been doing in them since birth. It is a function of how well we know them—the passions, gifts, and interests already at work in their lives. We are able to picture this future for them because we have been paying attention to the unique ways God has wired them.

The goal here is to express an expectation of success and accomplishment. It has nothing to do with worldly gain or a career choice we may wish them to pursue. Career has to do with what we are hired to do. Special purpose has to do with calling—how God has wired each of us, whether in the context of career or any other part of life. Our role as conduits of blessing is to acknowledge this wiring that God is gradually revealing. In effect, we are saying to them, "I believe in you and expect you to succeed in the special purpose God has planned for you as His workmanship." The blessing encourages the cultivation of those things God is already doing.

Word pictures are a powerful way to express what God is doing. For example, I might say, "God has given you a special ability to attract others to yourself and be a leader among your peers." A more powerful way of saying the same thing would be something like, "People appear to be drawn to you like birds to a birdfeeder. May God make you a wise, humble leader who shares His blessings and turns the spotlight from yourself to God and others." The words we use in the blessing must communicate truthfully.

The next element is equally important for communicating to the recipient of the blessing the authenticity of the message spoken.

# element #2: meaningful touch connection

The subject of touch poses some complicated challenges in today's culture, especially when it involves children and members of the opposite sex. Men are particularly subject to suspicion in this area. Concerns about inappropriate touch only exacerbate an already-common reluctance of men in our culture to engage in physical expressions of affection.

Adding to the confusions is the unwritten code among macho males that it is not 'manly' to hug. This can make anything more than a handshake uncomfortable for many. Some fathers are uneasy touching or hugging their sons once they become teenagers. In spite of this cultural imprint, it is encouraging to see more and more men throw off the hugging straightjacket imposed by society. I love seeing a man embrace his sons and others with appropriate affection. Obviously, for many men, this is still an awkward act. The risk of being misunderstood still looms large in men's minds.

In most Middle Eastern cultures, physical touch is a normal means of relating. The idea of men hugging and kissing other men may seem strange to Westerners, but not so in many parts of the world. Whether it is culturally normative or not, physical touch is a critical piece for any meaningful relationship. It is also a very important component of the spoken blessing. Without touch, a powerful element for connecting the affections of our heart in the spoken message is diminished.

Psychological research has long trumpeted the vital importance of touch to express and sometimes intensify personal emotions, feelings, and reactions. The long-term detrimental effects of touch deprivation on human beings are significant, especially in the emotional and relational development of a child. Children are severely and negatively affected by the deprivation of touch in their families. Often, the absence of this basic human need can produce a lifetime of dysfunction.

A child deprived of meaningful touch will often spend the rest of their life reaching for someone else's touch. Evil predators readily detect the scent of those robbed of affection in family relationships. Parents who have adopted children from orphanages where personal touch was missing or mostly expressed in negative forms know the impact those conditions have on a child.

We were meant for touch. Notice that Jesus did not simply *speak* words of blessing when He called the children to Himself. In the gospel of Mark, we are told that Jesus *"took them [children] up in his arms, **put his hands upon them and blessed them"** (Mark 10:16). Touch is an important means of reinforcing a sense that we are truly loved and valued for who we are, not what we do.

As an accompaniment to words of blessing, our words are imbued with a power that authenticates the message in the mind and the heart. Like a kiss when we say, "I love you," meaningful touch adds a 'wow-factor' to our words of blessing. Either words or touch may be meaningful by themselves at times, but when knit together in an act of genuine compassion they deeply affect a child's (and adult's) heart. Touch acts like a sprinkler system valve opening the way for the flow of life-giving words into the pipeline that connects to the heart. God wants us to be that pipeline—the delivery system for His water of life to a thirsty heart.

Our Creator meant for us to engage in relationship this way. That is why the curse of sin is so devastating in our relationship with God. We lost the touch and intimacy with the One who made us for Himself. The restoration of that intimate touch is why the Gospel is such good news. Through Christ's love expressed on the cross, God reached down, touched our deadness, and made us alive in Him. The intimacy we were created to enjoy with our heavenly Father can now once again become a reality.

Our goal is to speak blessing into their lives. Check your heart. Be wise, humble, and gracious in every act. Inappropriate touch will destroy the blessing you want them to receive. [See the Chapter Notes (#2) for comments about appropriate touch in today's world.]

Remember, grandparents, while you are in a powerful position to bless your family members, if you are uncertain about how they may respond to a particular way of touching, ask them. Ask, *Will it be all right if I put my arm around you as I speak a word of blessing to you?* Or you might ask, *May I hold your hand while I speak these words of blessing over you?* If they say no, then find a different, more appropriate form of physical touch that will free that person to respond positively. It is not often that family members will resist being touched when they know it is sincere and that you are sensitive to their feelings. When you have established a reputation of trust, you are positioned to be conduit of God's blessing.

# element #3: active commitment

Our children and grandchildren need and want our blessing, but they also need to know that we stand behind what we say. When they know that we will be walking alongside them in the journey ahead, they will put more stock in what we say. As important as the words and physical connection are to them, if that is as far as it goes, it will mean very little in the long run. A failure to follow through with an *active* involvement in the fulfillment of the blessing will likely negate any positive message we may have communicated verbally.

Knowing that you are there for them and actively engaged in their lives will validate and awaken the reality of the blessing. Your active commitment to them will serve as a constant reminder of the truth that they are loved and valued. When a child knows you believe in him because your life validates your words, a heart is stirred to life. It is then that the possibility exists to see that child become all God intended for him to be. What better gift could be given? Let me insert a few words of caution here: Active commitment is not pestering your grandchildren or imposing your agenda on them. Neither does it mean elevating your kids and grandkids to the central preoccupation of your thoughts and life. Nor does an active commitment require that we be physically present throughout their life to be effective.

Active commitment means staying connected, taking a keen interest in their world, celebrating the milestones in their life, listening well, and engaging in heart-to-heart communication. Give them proper respect— honor them for who they are. Show them what it means to value, respect, and honor others as well.

Graciously enter their world without trying to force them to live in yours. Don't try to be their buddy. They don't need a crony or another BFF (Best Friend Forever). They need a wise, godly, and transparent confidant who will listen and help them navigate the world in which they live. They want to know that you are committed to helping them succeed. They want you to live up to what you say you believe about them and God's special future for them. If you do, you will establish a legacy of blessing for generations to come.

What is the practical process for establishing a legacy of blessing in your family? The next chapter will offer some specific guidance.

# food for thought and discussion:

Read Genesis 1:27-28; Numbers 6:22-27

- What is the purpose of blessing? What did God mean when He said that the blessing puts "His name" on His people?

- Can you identify the three elements of the blessing discussed in the chapter? Discuss the significance and importance of each of these in a child's or adult's life.

- Have you ever received a spoken blessing yourself? If not, how might that impact your ability to give your children and grandchildren what they most need?

# action steps:

- If anyone in your group has never been the recipient of a spoken blessing, someone in your group should step up and bestow a blessing upon that person as the Father's cherished treasure.

- Talk to your church leaders about the importance of the spoken blessing, and ask them to explore with you ways that void could be filled in your congregation.

- Stand together in a tight circle with hands touching the shoulders of the person next to you. Allow your group leader to speak a blessing over you.

# speak the good word

*"The Christian ought to be a living doxology."*
Martin Luther

When Diane and I were first introduced to the concept of the family blessing, our children were grown and starting their own families. I remember picking up Rolf Garborg's book, *The Family Blessing*, and feeling a little angry that no one had told me about this amazing tool when my daughters were growing up. I wondered what special blessings they might have missed because I did not know about this gift God provided to parents for their children.

We decided it was not too late to find opportunities to speak blessing over our kids. Now we also had an opportunity to develop a tradition for our grandchildren. We began with the blessings at birth and have continued to establish a blessing tradition in our family in several different ways. I encourage you to do the same for your family.

If you are part of a church community, you most likely have a tradition in your church of closing a weekend worship service with a benediction or blessing from your pastor. Our pastor always says, "Let me give you the good word." That's a great phrase. It is a "good word" because it expresses the Good News of God's grace, goodness, and continual presence in our lives. The tradition of speaking a "good word" as a benediction or blessing over a congregation has been around a long time. A great deal would be lost if the practice were stopped. Why not establish the same tradition in our families, like many Jewish families have been doing for generations?

There is no right or wrong way to establish a tradition of spoken blessing in your family. While the three elements of blessing outlined in the previous chapter ought to form the basic structure for your family blessing, how you present the blessing is up to you. It is limited only by your own creativity and effort. If you've never incorporated the spoken blessing in your family traditions, you may be unsure how to begin. Let me suggest two possible plans for making the blessing a new feature of your family tradition.

## the general blessing

As we learned in the previous chapter, the Bible records God's instructions to Moses regarding the speaking of a common blessing over all the people of Israel in Numbers 6.

"Tell Aaron and his sons, 'This is how you are to bless the Israelites. Say to them:

> "The Lord bless you and keep you;
>
> The Lord make His face shine upon you, and be gracious to you;
>
> The Lord turn his face toward you, and give you peace."'"

This corporate blessing became a pattern for speaking blessing upon individuals as well as a group of people for many generations. Unfortunately, somewhere along the way Christians never really incorporated it in the teaching of the church. The failure to speak blessing upon our children may partly explain why our prisons are overflowing and why we have so many epidemic addictions in our society. Deprived of blessing, many are looking in dangerous and destructive places to find it.

The general blessing is a simple, powerful tool for laying a solid foundation of blessing in your family. It utilizes two of the three key elements discussed previously. The only element not specifically addressed in the general blessing is the personal, active commitment. There's no reason it cannot be easily incorporated. When we examine the personal blessing, you will see that it is a more critical component.

As a general blessing, the Numbers 6 model expresses the high value God places on His people. God uses word pictures, such as, "His face shine upon you." The phrase, "the Lord turn His face toward you" (also translated in some versions, "The LORD lift up His countenance on you"), is a powerful picture of God's intentional attention to His children who are so precious to Him. (See Numbers 6:24-26.)

Meaningful touch was usually expressed by the laying on of hands. In the case of a large group, the raising and extending of the arms and hands over the group depicted God's anointing touch upon them.

In addition to these elements, I want to unpack three other significant aspects of God's blessing that are implicit in this general blessing. Before I do, allow me to repeat something I stated earlier: The spoken blessing is a powerful way to regularly and frequently communicate important truths about God's personal care and favor on a child or adult. Some families speak it over their children every night. Many grandparents speak it over their grandchildren every time they come to visit or after a long-distance phone call. How often you do it is not as important as doing it when the opportunity presents itself. Just make the commitment to do it.

As we dissect the three facets of the general blessing as found in Numbers 6, imagine how this type of spoken blessing might be used with your grandchildren, your children, and other groups (a Sunday school class or a small group you lead, for example).

# singing in the dark

## facet #1- God's protection
*The Lord bless you and keep you...*

In a world that can often feel very unsafe and uncertain, God wants us to know that He is Emmanuel, *God with us*. He will never leave us or forsake us. This part of the family blessing expresses the hope and confidence we have in God to protect us no matter how tumultuous, dangerous, or fearful our circumstances.

When I was a small child, my father would sometimes take me, along with my siblings, camping in a place called Vedauwoo (pronounced 'vee-da-voo'), Wyoming. It was a fun place with large mountains of granite rocks surrounding several campsites and picnic areas. During the daytime it was fun to climb the rocks and explore caves formed by piles of huge boulders. As children we felt very safe and unconcerned about the dangers of these adventures. My parents, on the other hand, felt a little more apprehension about us falling off high rocks. For us, it was a child's paradise.

At night, however, things took on a very different feel for me. As the darkness enshrouded our campsite, the only light available was our camping lantern. On a cloudless night the stars hung like suspended diamonds glimmering across the sky, but they provided little light to chase the fright away. Even with a bright moon, as a young child I found little comfort in its soft, eerie light.

The outhouse, an important resource for camping trips, was located no short distance from our campsite—at least from the perspective of a small boy. The path to the outhouse passed through a grove of trees near a creek. No matter how badly I needed to go, I could not be convinced to walk that path in the dark alone, even with a lantern. Who knew what lurked in those bushes along the path?

Fortunately, my father always came to the rescue. With the lantern in one hand, my hand in his other, we would walk down that path together. Sometimes he would whistle or sing a tune. It was usually a song from Johnny Appleseed, "Oh, the Lord is good to me..." In the midst of the darkness, I knew I was safe because my father was there with me, hand in hand, singing in the dark, which is even better than singing in the rain!

The parent or grandparent who speaks blessing into a child's life provides the equivalent of a song in the darkness. In those moments, a child will know he or she is in good hands. They will understand through your touch and words of blessing that the Father is with them—their hand in His—as He sings His song of love that drives out all fear.

# under God's umbrella

## facet #2—god's pleasure
*The Lord make His face shine upon you, and be gracious to you ...*

The grace of God is the ultimate expression of His pleasure with us, not because of anything we have done, but because it is His nature. The idea of His face "shining upon us" is another way of saying that God smiles—even laughs—because of us. To live under His pleasure is to enjoy His smile, knowing that He is pleased. It is to discover that in His pleasure we find our deepest pleasure. For the child (or adult) who lives under the umbrella of God's grace, there is no greater delight than to know that His smile reflects the pleasure He takes in being gracious to us.

People understand the power of a smile. Even people we don't know can make a positive impact on us through a smile. When someone we love smiles at us, the effect is dramatic. The smile of a parent or grandparent upon a child can often change that child's countenance and reaction to the circumstances around her. This important component of the family blessing is the cornerstone because it reinforces the high value God places upon His children and reveals the deep delight of His heart towards us in Christ.

# his full attention

## facet #3—god's peace
*The Lord turn his face toward you and give you peace...*

I was sitting across from someone I know in a coffee shop talking about something I thought was important and how it was affecting me. As I talked, my friend's eyes constantly darted back and forth between me and other people coming and going in the shop. At one point he fixed his attention on someone he knew who had just entered the coffee shop.

Our conversation was suddenly interrupted as he waved and signaled to this person to come to our table. Standing to greet him, my friend introduced me to his friend. He then invited him to join us. Our one-on-one conversation was abruptly concluded. His attention was now diverted from my unfinished story—and me—to something else. I felt ignored and unimportant.

When God turns His face toward you, His complete attention is directed to you. He is never distracted. As the Creator of the universe, He directs His full attention to you because He truly cares and wants you to know how much of a treasure you are to Him. His longing is to bless you by heaping His favor upon you.

After the Fall, God had no choice but to turn His face away from all mankind. The glorious truth of the Gospel is that, through the cross, He has once again turned His face toward those who respond to His invitation to come under His umbrella of grace and receive His favor. While His smile expresses His delight in us, His face turned or lifted towards us conveys His careful *attention* to us. That is truly amazing grace!

His grace means His favor, and that means you have His full attention. All the resources of heaven are at your disposal to accomplish His grand purposes through you. Among the resources God makes available to those of us called by His Name is His peace—His shalom. Shalom is knowing that God is seeking your highest good—your well-being. This is peace that transcends understanding. Now that is a real blessing! (See Appendix for some samples of general blessings.)

# the personal blessing

The personal blessing represents another dimension of spoken blessing that differs from the general blessing in that it directs its attention to an individual. The personal blessing invokes specific words of blessing intended only for that individual. It is similar to the patriarchal blessings that carried explicit messages related to God's purposes for a child.

The blessing of the patriarchs expressed a prophetic anointing of God to carry forward the covenants of God through His chosen people. The personal blessing discussed here expresses a similar but distinctive purpose. Like the patriarchal blessing, it is a verbal confirmation of God's unique purposes attached to a specific individual to be fulfilled through that individual's story.

Perhaps a description of some of the contexts for such a blessing will help to clarify. Here are two possible venues for speaking a personal blessing into the life of a child or grandchild. You'll find some examples of these blessings in the Appendix as well.

## venue #1: *milestones*

Milestones represent those once-in-a-lifetime events that occur in every person's life and warrant special acknowledgment. Milestones are an opportunity to continually reinforce the special future God has in store for that person. They mark particular stages of an individual's life and how God is shaping that person for His purposes.

Diane and I have been privileged to be physically present for each of the births of our grandchildren. Our desire was to start them on their life journey with a blessing. We wrote out and framed a special blessing for each of the grandchildren. Then we spoke it over them in the presence of the parents before they left the hospital.

When my fourth grandson, Daniel, was born, I was unable to be there the day of his birth. Diane was there, but I arrived the day after. Our daughter, Alisa, was scheduled to leave the hospital with Daniel the day I arrived. When it appeared that I might not get there at the time she was scheduled to be released, she informed the nurses that she and her baby would not be leaving the hospital until her son's grandfather arrived to speak the grandparents' blessing over him.

By God's grace I arrived just in time. We held little Daniel as we gathered in that hospital room. I had the privilege of speaking the blessing Diane and I had written especially for him, just as we had done with his two older brothers.

At various other milestones, including spending time with our grandkids at GrandCamp each summer, we again write specific blessing for each of our grandchildren. These express the high value and special future God is unfolding for each child. As we watch them grow, we learn more about how God has wired them and is shaping them for His purposes. They always look forward to those times of blessing.

As you consider ways you can speak personal blessing specifically into the lives of each of your grandchildren (don't forget your adult children and spouses), here are some possible milestone "markers" that represent momentous opportunities for doing so:

**Milestone 1:** Birth/Adoption

**Milestone 2:** Starting School

**Milestone 3:** Salvation and Baptism

**Milestone 4:** Adolescent Transitions—*Purity and Self-Control*

**Milestone 5:** Rites of Passage—*Childhood to Adulthood*

  (*In the pattern of the Jewish Bar-Mitzvah or Bat-Mitzvah*)

**Milestone 6:** Graduation from High School, College, or Trade School

**Milestone 7:** First Job or Career

**Milestone 8:** Courtship and Marriage

**Milestone 9:** First House

**Milestone 10:** A Promotion

**Milestone 11:** Major Accomplishment (*book published, award, etc.*)

**Milestone 12:** Retirement/Change of Career

## venue #2: *blessable moments*

God gave Moses specific instructions to parents and grandparents for maximizing teachable, *blessable* moments. These are recorded in Deuteronomy 6:7 (NASB) – *"You shall teach them [God's commandments] diligently to your [children] and shall talk of them when you sit in your house and when you walk by the way and when you lie down and when you rise up."* These teachable moments are also blessable moments. They describe the natural, daily routines of life where opportunities present themselves to dialogue and speak blessing into young lives.

If you are a long-distance grandparent, you can do this too. These opportunities are just as relevant for you as for those who live nearby or who live under the same roof with their grandchildren. Geographical separation does not obviate the application of this command. It does, however, necessitate intentionality and creativity.

The point of this instruction from the Lord is to remind parents and grandparents of their responsibility to live intentionally. A teachable moment is when you have the opportunity to talk about life, God, and eternity. A *blessable* moment uses these same opportunities for engaging in meaningful conversation to also speak words of blessing at a very personal level. It's a timely opening for anointing your children or grandchildren with powerful words that speak of their high value and God's special favor.

Unfortunately, many American families overlook these opportunities. A typical family today is filled with so much activity and distractions that these blessable moments are lost as we pass each other like ships in the fog. Grandparents, this is a perfect opportunity to fill the void. It doesn't matter whether you are a nearby or a long-distance grandparent. You can take advantage of blessable moments if you look for them.

Consider these typical *blessable moments* described in Deuteronomy 6:7-9.

# when you *sit in your house*

These are the moments when the family is gathered either formally or informally. It can be in the home or any place where you are together and have opportunity to come apart from the daily buzz of life to just sit and talk. Mealtime is the most obvious 'sit-down' moment. Unfortunately, few families have undistracted sit-down mealtimes together; or if they do, they are rare. Grandparents can step into this gap and by example encourage the restoration of intentional family times at the table. Meals aren't the only ways families can sit together and enjoy 'table talk,' however. Here are a few more opportunities to consider:

- **Family game times, movie nights, or Wii tournaments:** When your activity is over, why not sit down together and talk about what was enjoyed most and why? Conclude with a special blessing for each member of the family.

- **A family reunion:** Plan some sit-down moments in the schedule to talk about family history, amusing stories, and lessons learned. Include a family blessing ceremony to wrap up the time together.

- **Plan a time to go to a restaurant, movie, or other special event:** Afterwards, grab a soda or ice-cream cone and talk about the experience. Look for a chance to affirm a quality you see in them in the form of a blessing.

- **Telephone or email conversations:** Speak or write a word of blessing. If no one answers a phone call, leave a message with a special blessing.

- **Make some good use of the amazing internet tools available:** Skype, for example, is a great way for long-distance grandparents to enjoy a 'sit-down' moment with their grandchildren and adult children. Don't forget to end with a special word of blessing.

## when you *walk by the way*

Americans do not walk as much as past generations did. We much prefer driving, flying in an airplane, or using some form of public transportation. Most people would agree that Americans could use a few more walking activities. So now is a good time for us to make the effort to do more of it.

Here are a few *walk-along* opportunities that can be turned into blessable moments. Invite your grandkids to join you on a walk or hike. Keep your eyes open to the beauty of God's creation and turn it into a word of blessing. For example, you might say something like, "Look at the magnificent colors in the trees this fall. It reminds me of the beauty of God's handiwork when He made you. May God always fill you with the wonder of His handiwork in all of creation, including how wonderfully you are made!"

When you witness an event or unusual situation when you're out and about, let it be a signal to stop and speak a word of blessing over someone along the path. When your grandchild sees you doing something so out of the ordinary, it becomes a powerful example of living a life of blessing.

Here are a few *walk-along* possibilities you can do with your grandchildren (or anyone else). I'm sure you will think of many more effective options:

- A walk through the neighborhood or the park

- A bike ride

- A hike in the woods, the mountains, along the beach, out in the desert, or any other nearby setting for exploring and enjoying God's creation

- Walking through the mall

- Walking through a museum or art gallery

## when you *lie down*

Bedtime is a great time to look back and talk about the events of the day, clear up issues, pray together, and otherwise explore some of life's lessons. It's a grand time to not only pray but to also speak the family blessing over a child.

You may not have regular bedtime opportunities as grandparents, but when you do get them, make them special moments with your grandkids. At the end of a chaotic and activity-filled day, this is a great time to unwind with the grandkids and let them know how special they are. It will also help drive away certain fears they may have as young children. They will cherish these moments always, even as adults. Here is an example of what you might say:

_____, *may the Lord bless you and keep you in His loving and safe arms tonight. May you rest in peace knowing that He is with you and guarding you with His perfect love, and making His face shine upon you.*

## when you *rise up*

More often than not the mood of the whole day is determined by the first few moments when everyone climbs out of bed. How you speak to your children and grandchildren in those moments can set the tone for everything that follows.

Unless you are raising your grandchildren or they are at your house for a sleepover, you may not have as many of these *rise-up moments* as parents do. There are, however, other ways you can engage *rise-up moments* with your grandchildren. Once again—it's all about intentionality. Here are a few practical ideas that may stimulate your thinking about a few of the *rise-up moments* we can enjoy as grandparents:

- Call once a week or once a month on a school day before they head off to school. Pray over them, speak a short blessing, and encourage them in their day.

- Make a blessing plaque to hang over their bed or on a mirror in their bathroom that they will see every day when they get up.

- For teenagers, send a text message each morning or a couple of times a week as they are heading off to school. Just say something like, "May God bless you and keep you today. May the Lord fill you with the wonder of His creation and His special love for you. We love you, too. Nana and Papa."

## in tune with the moment

Taking advantage of blessable moments is not about canned statements but spontaneous expressions. It is about being in tune with the moment so that you can be a conduit of God's blessing for your grandchild—or some other person God brings into your life. I often will use words from the Aaronic blessing in Numbers 6:24-26 as a framework from which I speak. That is a good pattern, but it is more important that what you speak comes from the heart.

My daughter recently left for a weekend tradeshow as part of her business. She needed a good income weekend to help pay off inventory expenses and bank a little extra money. Before she left, I simply put my arm around her shoulder and said, "May the Lord bless you and keep you; may He prosper the work of your hands and pour out His favor upon you this weekend; may He be gracious to you and fill you with His peace." That's all I said.

They did have a good weekend; one of the best weekends of the entire year. I can't take any credit for that, and I don't know if my blessing had anything to with the outcome. Speaking blessing is not a guarantee of financial success. On the other hand, do you suppose it might have reinforced God's goodness in my daughter's eyes?

Speaking words of blessing can be as simple as saying, "May the Lord bless you and keep you." Or it might reflect a special moment shared watching a spectacular sunset and saying, "As the beauty of this sunset displays the glory of God's handiwork, may the Lord make your life radiate the beauty of His glory in all you do."

God has designated you to be His blessing-giver. Speak blessing often and speak it well. Live up to the role of blessing-giver. If you do, your children and grandchildren will be blessed, and they will call you blessed.

# food for thought and discussion:

Consider the significance of each of the statements in the blessing of Numbers 6:24-26. How have you experienced those things from the Father? Do you think your children would be blessed to receive them from you?

What is the difference between the General blessing and the Personal blessing? Talk about some ideas for using each of these in your family.

# action steps:

- Develop a plan for implementing the practice of speaking blessing over your children and grandchildren using both the General and Personal (Milestone) blessings.

- Over the next two weeks, commit to share with each other how you are establishing a tradition of spoken blessing in your family.

- Pray for each other for wisdom and the courage to start a blessing tradition in your family and to share it with others in your church.

# leave a well-versed legacy

g r a n d p a u s e :
*"The Christian is bred by the Word, and he must be fed by it."*
William Gurnall

Caroline is an heiress to a very great fortune. She describes the incalculable wealth her grandparents had amassed and left to her this way:

"From the time I was a little girl my grandparents carefully chose their most valuable gemstones and gave them to me, one after another. It wasn't until years later that I realized they'd given me a priceless treasure. Today, I consider myself one of the richest women in the world. You can give your grandchildren the same inheritance. How?

"The psalmist said, 'The law from your mouth is more precious to me than thousands of pieces of silver and gold.' And in Proverbs we're told, 'Wisdom is more precious than rubies, and nothing you desire can compare with her.' My grandparents believed that. Their hearts were fully engraved with God's Word and they passionately passed it on."[1]

How "well-versed" is the legacy you are passing on to your grandchildren? Nehemiah knew the importance of the Word in keeping the Israelites from forgetting who they were and how great their God was. It was the Word of God's Law that exposed their own sinfulness and led them to weep and repent. It was the Word that filled them with rejoicing as Nehemiah reminded them that the "joy of the Lord is your strength." God's Word was to them words of life, hope, and purpose.

Notice that when Ezra read the Law, the people stood from daybreak to noon listening to it. That's six hours of nonstop Scripture reading! Quite a contrast from the typical sound-bite approach to Scripture reading we hear today in most churches, or even in our homes. The men, women, and children stood that whole time to hear God's Word. Why? They were hungry for the taste of truth. It probably also helped that their brains had not been programmed by visual media stimuli that reduces attention span. Nehemiah had laid a foundation for spiritual renewal among the people during the rebuilding, and now their hearts longed for a living Word from God.

What place does the Word have in your family life? Is it taught, learned, memorized, and *lived* in your life? The love of God's Word distinguishes true disciples from merely religious people. There is no greater treasure you can leave your grandchildren than God's Word hidden in their hearts. The Word will reveal the truth about God's love for them through Christ Jesus and keep them from sin. The Word combined with unshakable faith expressed through authentic worship opens the heart to the Gospel and the lavish grace of God for their salvation.

I love my work with the children in our church AWANA program. The mission of the program is to help children of all ages know Christ and serve Him unashamedly. Scripture memorization is the foundation of the program. While not all children are equally motivated to learn their verses each week, exposing them to Scripture and challenging them to memorize it plants seeds in their hearts for the rest of their lives. There is nothing more rewarding than watching kids who have grown up in the program demonstrate the power of God's Word that's still deeply seeded in their hearts.

Some of you may have grandchildren who are not particularly motivated to memorize Bible verses. I have one or two like that. Perhaps you have grandchildren as I do who have learning challenges. For them, memorization of complex and abstract thought is extremely difficult. How do we help our grandchildren learn Bible verses if they fall into one of these categories? I'm not an expert, but here are some things I have learned.

## memorization tips

I enjoy occasional work in community theatre and church drama. I often hear people complain about having difficulty memorizing lines or lyrics to songs. I sometimes struggle with it myself. As a choir director for almost thirty years, I used to hear a litany of excuses why choir members could not memorize a particular piece of music. Most people will tell you that they have poor memories or difficulty memorizing things. Obviously, this age of information inflation does stretch our memorization abilities and motivation. But is memorization really that difficult for the average person?

For most of human history, man depended upon memorization to transfer information from one person or generation to another. Before the printing press, few people had access to written documents or books that they could read for themselves. They depended upon their memory to record what they heard so they could ponder it or pass it on to others.

With all the printed materials available to us today and the technological mediums through which we gather information, memorization is not as valued in society as it once was. Calculators and the internet, in fact, have contributed to diminished memory skills in America. We have become wholly dependent upon digital devices to store most our information.

To be fair, there is far more information being dumped upon us today than at any other time in human history. It has been estimated that there is more information in one issue of a major metropolitan newspaper than a person would encounter in an entire year in the 1600s. Throw in email, the internet, blogs, e-books, smart phones, and social networking, and you get some idea of the quantity of information bombarding our minds every day. With all this information so readily accessible, we seem to have much less need for recall and memorization.

Yet, in spite of the information overload most of us experience, we still memorize a great deal of information. For example, how many phone numbers have you memorized? I'll bet you know your social security number and perhaps your spouse's too. Think about other long numbers you've memorized such as bank accounts, addresses, safe combinations, etc.

Most of us quickly memorize what is interesting and important to us. Vast amounts of facts and procedural steps are memorized by scientists, engineers, computer geeks, lawyers, doctors, accountants, politicians, and law enforcement officers, to name a few. Sports writers and commentators easily memorize large amounts of boring statistics about teams and individual players. The problem is not our inability to memorize. It is our motivation.

Some children will be easily motivated to memorize Scripture with you. Most, however, will need a little coaxing. Your enthusiasm for the Word of God will help influence their eagerness to learn as well. Here are a few suggestions for cultivating a well-versed legacy with your grandchildren, some borrowed from Caroline Boykin's book, *The Well-Versed Family: Raising Kids of Faith Through (Do-Able!) Scripture Memory*.[2] She offers many excellent suggestions and proven tools for memorization.

## live up to the challenge

Let's be honest. We all need some incentives for doing most things in life. Sure, there are many things we do just because they must be done, whether we like it or not. You will not, however, find much success with your grandchildren by forcing them to memorize Scripture verses if they have no desire to do so. I believe in providing certain appropriate incentives as a means of encouraging my grandchildren to memorize, but I can't force it. My primary objective is to help them to learn and hide God's Word in their hearts. I will consider almost any effective way to motivate them to do that.

Having said that, recognize the difference between providing incentive and bribery. Offering your grandson $100 to learn a few verses is bribery. Rewarding your grandchild with an outing to one of their favorite places after achieving a goal for memorization is an appropriate use of incentive. The goal is not merely Scripture memorization, but also a love for God's Word. The outcome we are seeking is to deposit God's Word in a child's heart where it may become a guide to truth and right choices throughout life.

Here are a few suggestions from Caroline's book along with a few others that I believe will help cultivate enthusiasm for memorizing Bible verses:

- Select verses that are age appropriate. In most cases you cannot expect a five-year-old to memorize long, complex verses that a teenager may struggle to learn. Even for older children, start out with short, simple verses that are easy to memorize.
- Discuss with them what the verses mean as they are learning them. Ask questions and share stories about how the verse or passage impacted your life.

- Make sure you are learning the verses with them. Don't expect them to enthusiastically learn Bible verses you are making no effort to memorize.

- Forget the verse references for younger children. I work with kindergarten, first grade, and second grade children in our AWANA program. We are encouraged to always have the kids learn the references with their verses. I have found that kindergarten and first graders have a great deal of difficulty with that. If I put too much emphasis on the book, chapter, and verse number, they get distracted from the main objective of memorizing the verse. Even some of the book names, like Thessalonians, are very hard for many young children to pronounce, much less memorize. As much as possible, encourage them to learn the name of the book where the verse is found, but what is most important is to learn the verse and what it means.

- Develop creative approaches to make the learning and memorization something they look forward to doing. Use all your creative skills to find ways to motivate them to memorize. If you're baking cookies with the grandkids, or building a birdhouse, use the time to say verses together. Create some games and fun challenges as part of the learning process. You could turn it into a charades game, and see if they can figure out what the verse is you are acting out.

- Develop fun and effective incentives for memorizing. You might set up a point system for each verse they learn. After so many points have been earned, they can use them to purchase items from Nana and Papa's General Store. Special outings, fun activities, or craft projects could also be incentives for learning verses.

- My friend and author, Renée Gray-Wilburn, offers a very wise suggestion. "I think it is really important that young children should only focus on one verse to memorize per week. Otherwise it becomes an overload for them. They need time to not only memorize, but process the verses and put them into practice." Good advice, Renée!

I know one grandfather who has established an annual tradition for their family reunion involving all the kids and teens. A list of suggested memory verses is given to them before they arrive at the reunion. He offers each child one dollar for every verse on the list they memorize and can explain in their own words by the end of the reunion. The kids come fully prepared and ready for the payoff. Grandpa delights in seeing them learn verses and talk about what they mean. Even the older teens look forward to the challenge each year.

While this could be construed as bribery, the fact that a very small that a very small amount of money is involved and nearly every grandchild is learning Scripture may well justify the means in this case. Did I mention that to get the dollar they also have to explain what the verse says in their own words?

# write it down

A well-versed legacy involves more than memorizing Bible verses. Clearly, that which authenticates and impresses God's Word into the hearts and minds of our children and grandchildren is an authentic life. Once we are gone, however, what will keep the legacy alive for the generations that follow? It is how powerfully God's truth was lived out in our lives.

Writing down our stories and the lessons we have learned in life is another great way to preserve that well-versed legacy for other generations. The Bible provides some amazing stories of great men and women of faith from Abraham to Esther to Jesus and the apostles. Their stories, the stories of extra-biblical men and women of faith, and our own stories strengthen another generation's resolve to face the challenges of life with confidence in God's grace. Our story is important not only for today, but also for future generations who need to be well-versed in the history of God's faithfulness expressed through their own family tree.

My wife, Diane, started a process of creating a memory book of personal stories from her life to pass on to our daughters and grandchildren. She got the idea from a dear friend of ours, Lana Rockwell, who has written about how to pass on a written legacy.[3] Each year Diane adds new pages to the story book she started. Our daughters consider it one of their cherished possessions. Besides providing meaningful insight into their mother's life, it also helps them understand how her story has shaped their own. Our stories are assets that need to be preserved so they can be handed down to the next generations as a source of blessing.

The Christian Grandparenting Network's *Legacy Journal* is another tool for recording your stories for future generations. The first part of the Journal provides help for writing down important facts about your family tree and relevant details about your own lives. The second part is dedicated to sharing your personal thoughts and experiences related to important issues of life. Some of those issues listed include thoughts about life and death, marriage and family, building character, career choices, faith, and politics. The final section provides space for writing a personal blessing for the recipient of the Journal. You can find more information about this resource at www.legacyjournal.org.

It's time to reclaim the power of spoken blessing in a world filled with cursing. It's up to you whether you will build a well-versed legacy or a non-versed legacy. The ball is in your court. How will you play?

# food for thought and discussion:

Read Nehemiah 8:1-9; 9:1-6

- Can you imagine standing for six hours listening to someone read the Scriptures? Why is that so hard to imagine in our time? Where do you see examples of God's Word being highly valued in your own experiences?

- What are the excuses most typically used for not memorizing Scripture? How valid are these excuses?

- What are the obstacles you face to encourage Bible memorization with your grandkids? Discuss possible solutions to overcome those obstacles.

- Discuss together ways to make Bible memorization more delightful as well as ways to teach God's Word in everyday life.

- What steps are you taking to write down your stories to leave for the next generations? If you haven't done this, what is keeping you from doing it?

# action steps:

- Set up a challenge for you and your group to memorize Scripture. It could be one verse a week or a larger passage of Scripture over a period of time.

- Discuss ways to encourage Scripture memorization among your grandchildren.

- Pray for one another in this journey of Scripture memorization and writing down your stories. Stop to thank God for His Word and to help you hide it in your hearts and in the hearts of your grandchildren.

p a r t    s i x

# SIGN UP!

*"When I saw their fear, I rose and spoke to the nobles, the officials and the rest of the people: 'Do not be afraid of them; remember the Lord who is great and awesome, and fight for your brothers, your sons, your daughters, your wives and your houses.'"*
Nehemiah 4:14, NASB

*A delegation from the tribe of Judah, led by Caleb son of Jephunneh the Kenizzite, came to Joshua at Gilgal. Caleb said to Joshua, "Remember what the LORD said to Moses, the man of God, about you and me when we were at Kadesh-barnea. I was forty years old when Moses, the servant of the LORD, sent me from Kadesh-barnea to explore the land of Canaan. I returned and gave from my heart a good report, but my brothers who went with me frightened the people and discouraged them from entering the Promised Land. For my part, I followed the LORD my God completely. So that day Moses promised me, 'The land of Canaan on which you were just walking will be your special possession and that of your descendants forever, because you wholeheartedly followed the LORD my God.'*

*"Now, as you can see, the LORD has kept me alive and well as he promised for all these forty-five years since Moses made this promise—even while Israel wandered in the wilderness. Today I am eighty-five years old. I am as strong now as I was when Moses sent me on that journey, and I can still travel and fight as well as I could then. So I'm asking you to give me the hill country that the LORD promised me. You will remember that as scouts we found the Anakites living there in great, walled cities. But if the LORD is with me, I will drive them out of the land, just as the LORD said."*

*So Joshua blessed Caleb son of Jephunneh and gave Hebron to him as an inheritance. Hebron still belongs to the descendants of Caleb son of Jephunneh, the Kenizzite, because he wholeheartedly followed the LORD, the God of Israel.*
Joshua 14:6-14, NLT

# to the hill country

**g r a n d p a u s e :**

*"Nothing can cure us of fear till God cures us of unbelief."*

Francis Burkitt

**C**aleb, son of Jephunneh, is one of my heroes. He was the kind of man I want to be. He had a passion for living and a wholehearted commitment to believing and serving God no matter how dangerous that might be. You know his story. It happened long before Nehemiah—before the walls of Jerusalem, the Temple, and the kings of Israel.

Selected by Moses as one of twelve elite reconnaissance team members assigned to spy out the land God had promised to the Israelites, Caleb took his assignment seriously. After completing their exploration of the land, the twelve returned to report their findings.

About this much they were all in agreement—the land was indeed filled with abundant goodness just as God said. The amazing samples of the bountiful fruit they brought back confirmed God's promise of a land flowing with milk and honey.

Concerning the rest of God's promise, however, the team was not united. Overshadowing God's assurance that the inhabitants could be defeated were unmistakable realities staring them in the face. Not only were there a lot people, but they were huge, giant-sized people. Only Caleb and Joshua believed God and stood in opposition to the popular opinion expressed by the other ten. Ten of the twelve wanted to play it safe; two believed God would defeat their enemy. The trepidation of the ten spread like a plague throughout the camp of Israel, causing the people to cower in paranoia and panic.

Whoa, hold on there! Are we missing something here? Aren't these the same people who had recently witnessed incredible miracles of God since leaving Egypt? Hadn't they seen God part the sea for them so they could cross on dry ground? Weren't they the ones who stood safely on the other side of that sea and watched God unleash the parted waters to drown Pharaoh's pursuing army? Surely they had not forgotten the daily reminders of God's presence in the pillar of fire by night and a cloud by day. Hadn't they experienced God's goodness as He quenched their parched throats with water from the rock and satisfied their hunger with manna and quail? How can someone witness such amazing things firsthand and get hung up on a few oversized Anakites?

At any rate, the scouts made their report: *"The land we explored devours those living in it. All the people we saw there are of great size…we seemed like grasshoppers in our own eyes and we looked the same to them"* (Num. 13:32-33).

Their ability to accurately evaluate their circumstances in terms of who they were and who their God was had been blurred by fear driving them to unbelief. It was too radical a leap for them to believe God could do something this big, even though He had already proven Himself quite capable in big things. How short our memories can be.

From our vantage point of hindsight it's difficult to understand how, after all God had done getting them to this point, they couldn't trust Him to finish the job. After all, God appeared to Moses in the burning bush and gave him these promises: 1) He would rescue them from the hand of the Egyptians; and 2) He would bring them into a "good and spacious land, a land flowing with milk and honey." The "good and spacious land" now lay before them just as God had promised. Now they stood paralyzed, unwilling to take action to claim that promise.

Before we point fingers and shake our heads at these foolish Israelites, we might want to look in the mirror. I suspect there are a few giants in our lives that strike terror in our hearts and keep us from following God's call. Fear has a way of evaporating our confidence in God's promises. Sometimes it's easier to simply follow the crowd rather than stand up and do what is right.

If it's true that only 10 percent of a society holding an unshakable belief can lead that society to adopt its belief, then why has the Christian community been so impotent to impact our society? According to the Chuck Colson Center for Christian Worldview, less than 10 percent of Americans make up the cultural elite of our society—those we hear about, read about, and see in the media. Yet, grandparents who claim to be Christians in this nation make up considerably more than 10 percent of our population. Why are we not the cultural influence in our society? Is it possible for us to replace the influence of the postmodern cultural elitists? That depends.

If our faith in the God of Heaven is unshakable in every area of life, then we can become the primary cultural influence. If we live with a resolve not to be intimidated into silence, but to unite and stand up for what is right and true, we can be light in a world of darkness. So much depends upon how courageously we proclaim and live out the Gospel by the power of the Spirit with authenticity, compassion, and grace—seasoned, of course, with salt.

## ending the spiral of silence

We live in a time when the majority is often found cowering in silence as those who wield the power to shape public thought and policy bully their way through society using intimidation to substitute politically correct. The late Elizabeth Noelle-Neumann, German political scientist, referred to it as the "spiral of silence" in her famous work by the same title.[1] Her theory asserts that people are less likely to voice their opinion on a topic if they sense they are in the minority, especially if they fear some reprisal from the majority.

In other words, when the mass media spin their view of a particular social issue in order to shape public opinion on that issue, the majority will sit in silence once they perceive the matter has been decided, even if they disagree. Most people fear rejection or isolation from the mainstream. They will typically concede the issue rather than endure the stinging disapproval of society with the label of "bigot" or "hatemonger."

A 2009 study entitled, *The False Enforcement of Unpopular Norms,* at the University of California, Berkley, describes false enforcement as the pressure to conform to a norm not otherwise accepted.[2] This false enforcement is illustrated by the familiar Hans Christian Andersen fable, *The Emperor's New Clothes.*

In this well-known tale of a naked emperor, his tailors convince him that his new suit of clothes will be invisible to anyone in his realm who is stupid, incompetent, or unfit for his court. Not wanting to be labeled as such, his court goes along with the ruse and manipulates the masses to do the same, even though every one knows the truth. No one wants to risk speaking the truth for fear of reprisal by the emperor. That has a familiar ring to it.

Following the courageous example of the small child who finally spoke up and declared, "But he isn't wearing anything at all," it's time for this generation to speak up and tell the truth. We must wake up, wise up, and rise up to counter the delusion under which we have lived for too long. It may take a few courageous grandparents to lead the charge and tell the emperor he is naked. God has already declared that we have everything we need by His divine power for life and godliness (see 2 Peter 1:3). We do not have to be enslaved to the spiral of silence. We are free by the power of God to launch a movement that will speak out for the sake of our grandchildren and the glory of God.

Is speaking the truth risky and dangerous? Absolutely. Seemingly insurmountable obstacles and risks are part of life, especially when we are pursuing God's agenda. Wholehearted followers of Christ know that it is dangerous business. Fear is still our greatest enemy. It is constantly poised to warp our perspective of reality, numb our hearts, and intimidate us into silence. Fear dupes us into believing we can embrace a "safe faith"—whatever that means. Living out a genuine, unshakable faith is never safe, but it *is* right. God is faithful, trustworthy, and bigger than any danger we might encounter, and that is the reason we can take the risk.

It's time to shed the lie that we can play it safe and win. We need not fear those defining moments God sets before us. Our vision is not fixated on the dangers and risks involved. Rather, we *"fix on our eyes on Jesus, the author and perfecter of our faith, who for the joy set before him endured the cross"* (Heb. 12:2). This is the reason we do not grow weary or lose heart. Before us are amazing opportunities for God to display His glory and might. If fear wins, the next generations lose. Are you willing to allow that to happen on your watch? I'm not.

Worry, fear, anxiety—these are the things that shift our eyes from God to our circumstances. It was what Caleb had to battle with his cohorts. Nehemiah had to deal with it too as Sanballat and his co-conspirators attempted to intimidate the Jews trying to rebuild the wall. Nehemiah refused to be intimidated because he knew the Lord was fighting for him and the people. He reminded them of God's promise and why they were doing what they were doing. This was a struggle for their families and homes. The same is true for you and me today.

Perhaps you struggle with doubt seeping its way into your thoughts. You may find yourself asking, *What if I fail*? So what if you do? Someone once wisely said, "Failure is the context for miracles." If you never step out in faith and take a risk, you may delude yourself into thinking the safest route is the best choice. But it rarely is.

The safe path is, in fact, a dead-end path paved with fear and apathy. The intimidation tactics of the opposition will always paralyze you.  If you surrender to their intimidation you embark on a road that diverts you from the opportunity to show your family and the world the greatness of God. You will also allow the enemy to breach the defenses around your family.

That's what I love about Caleb. Caleb understood the risks. He chose to remain resolute in his belief that God is able to do what He promised He would do. He knew that, in spite of the dangers and obstacles, God had already promised to give them the land. He believed God.

Now, forty years later, Caleb stood before Joshua and asked for the land God had promised to him. His courageous, wholehearted commitment to God compelled him to boldly declare, "So *here I am today, eighty-five years old! I am still as strong today as the day Moses sent me out; **I'm just as vigorous to go out to battle now as I was then**. Now give me this hill country that the Lord promised me that day. You yourself heard then that the Anakites were there and their cities were large and fortified, but, the Lord helping me, I will drive them out just as he said"* (Joshua 14:10-11; emphasis mine).

I don't know about you, but when I read this, my response is "Wow"! Here was a man with a resolute, audacious, and deliberate belief that God would do what He promised no matter how big the obstacles seemed. Caleb wasn't interested in wasting his life by playing it safe. He was not afraid of danger. He was ready to do battle, even at eighty-five, because He believed God was bigger than any giant he might face and that there was too much at stake to sit and do nothing.

What battle is worth fighting today? We may not be sent into harm's way to fight terrorists like our brave young men and women in the military are asked to do. But we still have a battle to fight against a different kind of terrorism—a terrorism of truth. And like Caleb and Nehemiah of long ago, we too are fighting for our brothers, sisters, sons, daughters, husbands, wives, and homes. Grandparents, you are needed on the frontlines in this battle.

Our mission is to take back the hill country the enemy has gained on our watch. It does not matter if you are a long-distance grandparent, a grandparent raising your grandchildren, a new grandparent, or a grandparent with a quiver filled with grandchildren, you are being called back to active duty for another generation.

Boomers cut their teeth on activism. Now we have a cause more important than any cause I can imagine. We are being called for a final round of activism. This is a cause for truth and righteousness. It is a cause for the hearts and minds of our grandchildren. This is the point where the courageous do what is right. They sign up for the job of fighting for our homes and our country.

We cannot afford to play it safe and settle back into a comfortable retirement. To play it safe is to assume the greatest risk of all—a wasted life that leaves nothing of value to the next generations. John Piper put it this way: "If our single, all-embracing passion is to make much of Christ in life and death, and if the life that magnifies Him most is the life of costly love, then life is risk, and risk is right. To run from it is to waste your life."[3]

These are turbulent and uncertain times requiring radical solutions from a courageous people who hold to an unshakable faith in Jesus Christ. It is not a political battle in which intimidation and fear are our weapons of influence. Dr. Haddon Robinson, Distinguished Professor at Gordon-Conwell Theological Seminary, rightly said, "If we are committed to a 'cause' but remain unconcerned with Christ, we may trade away the power of God for the power of politics."

In Christ, we have weapons unlike any other. *"The weapons we fight with are not weapons of the world. On the contrary, they have divine power to demolish strongholds. We demolish arguments and every pretension that sets itself up against the knowledge of God, and we take captive every thought to make it obedient to Christ"* (2 Cor. 10:4-5).

Grandparents, your deployment orders have been issued. Will you sign up and step up as Christ's ambassadors and soldiers for the sake of the next generations? Understand what's at stake if you don't.

# food for thought and discussion:

- Read through Nehemiah 4. What was the nature of the opposition that Nehemiah and the people of Jerusalem faced in their task of building the wall? What is the nature of opposition we face today?

- How did Nehemiah face the opposition and rally the people to complete the task?

- Why do we fear speaking the truth in the public square today? Why is political correctness so dangerous and destructive? How do you respond to the notion that speaking the truth is risky and dangerous?

- Read 2 Timothy 3:1-5; 4:3-4. What does it look like to be "strong and courageous" in such times? Is it possible to change a culture that turns its back on the truth? Why or why not?

# action steps:

- Make a list of the things that create fear and discouragement in your life. Lay the list before God and confess your fears. Now ask Him to replace your fear with courage and resolve to do what is right and speak the truth boldly.

- Taking the hill country also involves linking arms with others who are willing to join the battle. Caleb did not go into battle alone. Using Paul's instruction in 2 Timothy 4:2, develop a strategy for engaging your families and your sphere of influence with the truth about the Gospel.

- Pray for one another as you step out in faith to be strong and courageous.

# where the rubber meets the road

*"Consecration is resolution that is not afraid of sacrifice."*
Anonymous

The story is told of a shoe manufacturer who sent two salesmen to an underdeveloped country to see about the prospects for expanding business there. One salesman emailed back to the home office, "Prospect here nil. No one wears shoes." The other salesman also emailed back, but his response showed a different perspective. He wrote, "Market potential enormous! Everyone is barefoot!"

Life is full of daunting barriers and obstacles. The idea of changing an entire culture can seem like an impossible task—like trying to sell shoes to a barefoot society! I challenge you to look for the opportunity and potential for change. Start by seeking the Lord and aligning your heart with His so you can see the possibilities before you. Then get up and fight for your sons, your daughters, your grandchildren, your spouse—fight for your homes.

Reformation is never easy. Few people understood that more than William Wilberforce. In the midst of overwhelming public opposition to his proposals to end the slave trade in England, Wilberforce began to speak and write and fight for what he knew to be true. Over the course of twenty-six years he campaigned relentlessly to abolish this horrific practice. His persistence and unshakable conviction of the rightness of his cause reshaped public opinion and ultimately led to the Abolition of Slavery Act of 1833. It happened because a courageous, determined man with an unshakable belief in God, God's call on his life, and justice for all men was undeterred in his commitment to see his cause through, regardless of public opinion.

Will you stand with other grandparents with the same resolute determination and the same unflinching belief in God's divine power to confront the lies and destruction imposed upon our society? The cause in which we unite is a Kingdom cause. We are engaging in a battle to set our children and grandchildren free from the grip of Satan's lies through the transforming power of the Gospel.

This is where the rubber meets the road. No more talk—let's go to work. What are we to do? Here are five suggestions for those who mean business:

1. **PRAY!** Pray privately in your own closet. Pray with other believers as well. If you aren't already part of a group of grandparents who are praying regularly for the next generations and our families, I challenge you to

organize one now in your area. CGN facilitates G@P (Grandparents At Prayer) groups to encourage grandparents to join together in prayer. Jesus said, *"Where two or three are come together in my name, there I am with them"* (Matthew 18:20).  Corporate prayer is powerful. When two or three or more unite their hearts with the Father's, the floodgates of Heaven are opened. Very little corporate praying happens in American churches today. Determined grandparents can change that, so let's do it. I also encourage you to get a copy of Lillian Penner's book, *Grandparenting with a Purpose: Effective Ways to Pray for Your Grandchildren*[1]. Revival is the fruit of fervent praying.

2.  **REPENT!** Praying is not merely petition. It is a time to allow God to search our hearts and expose any wicked ways or motives. Repentance means owning up to our sins, both individually and as a people. Courageous grandparents accept that responsibility because we know that personal and corporate revival originate in repentance. Repentance acknowledges that we have strayed from the truth and the paths of righteousness. It starts with us—dealing with the sin and rebellion in our own lives. But it doesn't end with confession. True repentance changes course and becomes the pipeline through which God's transforming power of grace and truth is unleashed in our culture.

    Once more Nehemiah sets an example for us. Upon learning of the condition of his homeland, he wept and went to his knees to confess the sins of Israel. He did this before he asked God's favor to win over the king. In the same way we must acknowledge our guilt. At times we have compromised when we should have stood our ground. We have remained silent when we should have spoken out. We have embraced a life of selfishness and greed when we should have looked to the interests of others, especially the poor. We are guilty of "dumbing down" the Gospel and allowing evil to weasel its way into our homes.

    When we humble ourselves and repent, God makes a promise: *"If my people will pray, and humble themselves, and turn from their wicked ways, then will I hear from heaven,"* says the Lord God (2 Chronicles 7:14). We would be foolish to allow pride to stand in the way of God's promise to pour out His blessing.

3.  **SPEAK OUT:** God will work through even a lone voice. That's what He did through men like Wilberforce and Wesley, Nehemiah and Caleb. How much more might God move in people's hearts when the voices of thousands upon thousands speak out to proclaim the truth? One way to speak out is to organize a *Courageous Grandparenting* group in your

community. Gather likeminded grandparents and parents to study God's Word, to pray, and to stimulate one another to be God's culture-makers for a time such as this.

Here are some other speak-out venues for truth and righteousness I urge you to consider:

Participate in the election process whenever possible. Attend a caucus that selects candidates for office. Let your voice be heard on issues that impact our nation, especially matters of morality, family, and sanctity of life. Don't let the intimidation tactics of others keep you from speaking out.

Communicate with your elected representatives. Remind them of their responsibility to the guard the general welfare of the people by enacting laws that align with the higher standards of God's moral law.

Sign the Manhattan Declaration at www.ManhattanDeclaration. org[2]. The Manhattan Declaration gives a voice to the masses that believe our nation is strong only when we hold to God's just and moral laws regarding life, marriage, and religious liberty. You can read the complete text online. Read it, sign it, and then ask your friends and neighbors to do the same. When you do, you are joining with hundreds of thousands of others who want to reaffirm their commitment to truth, righteousness, and compassion. The Manhattan Declaration graciously affirms our determination to stand upon truth and justice, even in the face of unjust laws.

It was Martin Luther King, Jr. who wrote from a Birmingham jail,

> *There are two types of laws; just and unjust… One has a moral duty to disobey unjust laws, for an unjust law is no law at all…. A just law is a man-made code that squares with the moral law or the law of God. An unjust law is a code that is out of harmony with moral law.*[3]

We are obligated to *"obey God rather than men"* (see Acts 5:29) when forced to choose between the two.

4.  **CONNECT INTER-GENERATIONALLY:** Courageous grandparents seek opportunities to intentionally engage with their grandchildren and other children, youth and young adults in their sphere of influence. Consider these possibilities:

    •   Get involved in the children's ministry in your church. I recently asked a group of senior adults to get involved in the children's ministry in their church once a month.

As you may have guessed, I got no takers to my invitation. I did get some responses along the lines of: "I already did my time when I was younger"; "I'm too old to work with kids. Leave that to the younger folks." Sound familiar?

At what age are we too old to contribute to a child's life? And who came up with the notion that raising kids or working with children is about 'doing time'? Ministry to kids isn't a prison sentence—it's an opportunity to joyfully live for something more important than our own convenience. It's a chance to be a conduit of God's grace for the next generations.

I'm involved with the AWANA program in my home church. It is one of the most rewarding things I do. Sure, it is challenging at times, but I love each of my thirteen first and second graders whom I see each week. I love sharing Bible stories and helping them memorize Bible verses.

- Take your grandchildren to GrandCamp (www.grandcamps. org) or create your own version of GrandCamp or Cousins Camp. Gwen, one of our regular GrandCamp grandparents, wrote me about their experiences at GrandCamp. "The Christian faith of our grandchildren is much deeper largely due to the experiences with us at GrandCamp. For example, after spending just two days at GrandCamp, one granddaughter exclaimed, 'Grandma, GrandCamp is so much fun, and it's so much FUN learning about GOD!'"

  Never settle for simply being a good grandparent! Choose to be a courageous, adventurous grandparent. You can be intentional and diligent about your family's well-being and eternal destiny. Invest in your grandchildren and spend time with them. Explore, debate, create, and serve together. If you are long distance, find a way to stay in touch regularly. There are lots of options available to you. (Reread Chapter 7!)

- Challenge the leadership of your church to promote more inter-generational dialogue and discussion events. For example, propose a weekend inter-generational retreat where you can sit down and discuss some of the social issues of our day and what God has to say about them. We tried this at a two Christian colleges a few years ago. We called it the Inter-Generational Institute. It was an amazingly significant activity for everyone involved.

- Reclaim the family table. I love the scenes in each episode of the TV series, Blue Bloods, when four generations of the Regan family sits down to dinner and engage in conversations about the stuff of life. This is not a pattern strictly for television. It's a tradition that ought to be part of every family. While it might not be possible for all of us to have four generations together all the time, we can still work to make the family dinner table an opportunity for inter-generational dialogue if we choose.

  A study out of Columbia University5 finds that teens who eat dinner with their parents five to seven times a week are four times less likely to engage in harmful activities like drugs and alcohol. It's also been shown to greatly reduce the incidents of teen suicides. Family dinners are not only good for bonding but for talking about values and sharing life together. That's almost always a good thing for any family.

  Dinner table traditions are becoming more scarce in the life of the modern American family. Everyone is going in different directions. Grandparents, you can set the example by insisting on sitting together at the table when the family visits sans cell phones and television. Encourage your adult children to do the same in their own homes. Once or twice a week is better than nothing. Everybody wins in this plan.

- Do The Right Thing: The Colson Center for Christian Worldview and the Witherspoon Institute have co-produced a DVD curriculum suitable for use with a small groups, a class, or even a family reunion. The series explores and examines matters of ethics and character that relate to home, school, and the workplace. It is a wonderful tool for inter-generational dialogue. Visit www.doingtherightthing.com for more information.

**5. BE GRACIOUS ALWAYS:** On matters of faith and morality do not be surprised when people are not receptive to civilized dialogue. In such situations, it is important to be a sincere listener and gracious communicator. James says that we are to be *"quick to listen, slow to speak and slow to become angry"* (James 1:19). That's a tall order when someone is shouting in your face and unwilling to allow your opinion to be voiced. Resist the temptation to respond in kind.

When dealing with hot topic issues like abortion, homosexuality, same-sex marriage, and so forth, earn the right to be heard by being a gracious listener and using kind words. Shouting matches or inflammatory picket signs do relatively little to change people's hearts or open up an opportunity for dialogue.

Your grandchildren need to know that they will not be condemned if they take a position on an issue you know is wrong. Let truth be seasoned with grace so the Spirit is free to do the work of conviction. Use questions to stimulate conversations and guide them to think about their position. Ask them to articulate why they take the position they do. Questions like, "Why do you think your position is the right position? Do you know what the Bible says about the issue? Does it matter to you? Why or why not?" produce more positive results than, "I can't believe you could believe something so obviously wrong!"

Challenge them to read and research differing points of view and apply critical thinking about what they learn. Offer to discuss the issues in question in the context of an open and kind dialogue.

Affirm their value as human beings made in God's image. Communicate your love whatever they choose to do. With gentleness and kindness also let them know that on matters in which the Scriptures are clear, you will stand upon the authority of God's Word.

## compassionate engagement

These five action steps are radical in many ways, but Life with a capital 'L' in which Christ lives in me is anything but cozy. Those who choose to embrace these action steps with courageous faith will position themselves to be Christ's conduits of grace and change in a powerful way.

While you may desire the greatest good for those you love, not all will want what you want. Expect opposition along the way from those who don't get it or don't want to get it. Let your charity remain steadfast always. Dr. Mark Young, President of Denver Seminary, said it this way: "Passionate belief must never eclipse compassionate engagement with those who do not see the truth as we see it."[5] Nor, I might add, for those who do not want to see the truth at all.

Our family has had to face this with a man who is very dear to us. Trevor (not his real name) is a self-proclaimed homosexual. A resident of New York, he announced his same-sex 'marriage' to his gay partner on Facebook. When some of the family and Christian 'friends' did not post congratulations to him on his page, he responded with some intense anger. He announced he was 'unfriending' all the hateful, negative people on his list who did not offer congratulations.

Attempts to respond to him graciously were not well received. In fact, he was clearly hostile. There was no desire on the part of those who did not agree with his chosen lifestyle to abandon the friendship. In fact, they were eager to continue it. Unfortunately, Trevor was not receptive to any position other than his own on the matter. In fact, conditions were laid out for any acceptable relationship on his part. Those who would affirm and support his same-sex marriage publicly would be welcome. All others would be cut off. No allowance was made for disagreement or a different point of view. It was all or nothing.

For some in our family, this was an experience very much like the death of a dear friend. Even after one final plea to not terminate the friendship, Trevor's demands remained firm. My daughter, who was quite close, responded very graciously and let him know that her friendship and love for him would never be tied to conditions, even if he felt otherwise. She could not, however, abandon her faith and convictions about God's moral law simply to meet his demands. She would remain a friend without conditions, welcoming any opportunity to reconnect. In the end, he had nothing else to say.

Nehemiah was no stranger to hostility and opposition. When faced with intense opposition, Nehemiah responded by going to God in prayer because he knew this was the Lord's battle. Armed with wisdom for the moment, he took the appropriate action to deal with the opposition and continue the work. His charge to the people was to "remember the Lord, who is great and awesome.... Our God will fight for us." With that perspective, they finished the wall in fifty-two days. Those who opposed them had nothing left to say.

Never rest or desert the fight because of opposition. I will not give up until I have done all that God asks of me to stir this generation of current and emerging Christian grandparents into courageous action. Imagine with me what an army of faithful grandparents could do in the power of the Holy Spirit to bring revival in this land and our families. Can you imagine?

I believe my assignment is to remind you and grandparents everywhere of what's at stake if we don't wake up and rise up in response to God's call to live for the next generations. I challenge you to take up the cause with me for our grandchildren's sake—for the sake of every child, teen, and young adult being taken captive to the Lie. May God open your eyes to the opportunity of your lifetime.

# food for thought and discussion:

- Review the five action steps listed in this chapter. Do you agree with them? Why or why not?

- How can you encourage one another to make these things part of your everyday living? Which ones pose the greatest challenge to you?

- What does it look like to be compassionately engaged in the context of your family, your workplace, and your neighborhood?

# action steps:

1. Spend some significant time praying for each other in these specific ways:

- Wisdom to know how to put into practice these actions steps, first in each other's families then also in the church.

- Courage to face opposition with grace and compassion but without compromise.

- Confidence that God will give you everything you need and will never leave you or forsake you in the journey ahead.

2. Discuss how you can begin to form a G@P (Grandparents At Prayer) group to meet regularly to pray for each other's grandchildren, families, schools and the world they live in.

# a time for new heroes
## *a challenge to grandfathers*

g r a n d p a u s e :
*"Men are God's method. The Church is looking for better methods;*
*God is looking for better men."*
E. M. Bounds

**A**s part of a small Midwestern church Christmas program, young Ben was asked some questions about his family and interesting things about himself. At one point, he was asked the question, "Who is your hero?" Without hesitation, he boldly proclaimed, "My dad!"

It concerns me to see some of the heroes that kids and teens identify with today. Many of the rock star and celebrity heroes in their lives promote values and attitudes that ought to alarm any parent or grandparent. Perhaps the reason some of these warped personalities have achieved hero status is because there are so few real heroes in their lives. Too many kids have no dads to be their heroes.

The importance of fathers and grandfathers in the lives of children can never be overstated, but it is often under-estimated by men. Talk to anyone in prison ministry and they will tell you that young men who grow up in homes without fathers are twice as likely to end up in jail as those who come from traditional two-parent families. According to Prison Fellowship, more than "seventy percent of juveniles in state-operated institutions come from fatherless homes."[1]

The void of godly, paternal influences in the home is seriously impacting our children. How does a boy learn what it means to be a man if a man is not in his life to teach him and show him? I am not minimizing the important role mothers play in a child's life. I am simply calling attention to the harsh fact that boys growing up without fathers are at a disadvantage and less likely to become responsible men in society. Why do we have so much difficulty accepting this truth?

The point is that lots of boys are growing up without fathers or engaged fathers. That is why I believe grandfathers are so vital to our families. It is time for some new heroes to step to the plate in our families. If you are a grandfather and your grandchildren do not have a father in their home, you can be that hero. I urge you to welcome that privilege and responsibility—for the sake of your grandsons and granddaughters.

Numerous sociological studies suggest that the lack of male role models extends the period of so—called 'adolescence' among young males. In other words, men in their thirties and even forties are still living with a self-centered, childish perspective on life and responsibility. It is understandable when no intentional male example is involved in their life to teach them what it means to be a man—not to mention a godly man. God is calling you to stand in the gap and help them be all they can be.

Part of the problem working against us is a blind acceptance—void of honest, critical evaluation—of the notion of adolescence as normative. The idea of adolescence never existed prior to 1904 when Dr. G. Stanley Hall invented the concept in his paper called *Adolescence*. I don't want to take the time to explore this fallacious notion about the teen years and beyond in this book. I encourage you to read Dr. Chuck Stecker's book, *Men of Honor/Women of Virtue*[2] and learn more about the damaging consequences of this lie on the lives of our children as the enter adulthood.

Nowhere does the Bible even suggest such a stage of life like adolescence. Paul wrote, *"When I was a child, I talked like a child, I thought like a child, I reasoned like a child. When I became a man [adult], I put childish ways behind me"* (1 Corinthians 13:11). For most of human history societies had specific rites of passage processes for moving a child from childhood to adulthood. There was no notion of an in-between stage where a person was neither. This has become a great curse upon our children and society.

At nearly every event I do for the Christian Grandparenting Network, whether a conference, a seminar, or a prayer meeting, grandfathers are either conspicuously absent or poorly represented. The one exception is our GrandCamp programs. I love seeing these men engaging with their grandchildren at a deeper level than just having fun. These are not deadbeat grandfathers. They get it. I pray you are a grandfather who gets it too.

## no deadbeat grandfathers

In spite of these godly men I know, I am concerned that so many grandfathers miss the significance of their roles. I know there are more grandmothers living than grandfathers, but that doesn't explain the silent absence of men who should be taking up the battle for the hearts and souls of their grandchildren. To do that a man must know what it means to be a man of God and how to teach it to another generation.

When my oldest grandson turned fourteen, I saw an opportunity to partner with his father to begin a journey of discovery about manhood. A number of years ago I read a book by Robert Lewis, entitled, *Raising a Modern-Day Knight*. I don't have sons, but that book challenged my heart and stirred my spirit to consider what I need to do to help my grandsons grow up into authentic manhood. I recently read another author, Bob Schultz, who wrote *Boyhood and Beyond: Practical Wisdom for Becoming a Man*. Both these books challenged me to develop a strategy for coming alongside my sons-in-law to help guide my grandsons towards manhood.

This past year we spent two days together working through passages from the Word of God. We borrowed some of the creative ideas these authors suggested to explore what it means to be a man. I plan to employ a similar process with all my grandsons as they enter their teen years. I am committed to walk with them and their fathers through this rite of passage towards manhood.

Our goal is that by the time they each graduate from high school, they will understand four principles of manhood, will have demonstrated a commitment to living out those principles, and will be prepared to step out on their own into the world as a responsible man of God. I look forward to a special initiation ceremony to celebrate their entry into manhood, and to confirm my commitment to stand shoulder to shoulder with them as long as I am on this earth.

Unlike the United States, most societies practice rites of passage for men and women to mark their transition from childhood to adulthood. In the Western world, such rites, especially for boys, are less common. I think it's time to restore the rites of passage process in our families. I believe it will pay rich dividends as boys learn what it means to be men who treat women with respect and who model godly living.

My friendship with Chuck Stecker, founder of *A Chosen Generation,* has further motivated me to think about the process of rights of passage and understand God's design, not only for my sons and grandsons but for my daughters and granddaughters. Grandfathers, you must hold the standard high for you family. Wave the flag of truth, and march into battle for the hearts and souls of your families.

I applaud the courageous mothers who bear the incredible burden of raising children in a home devoid of a father or appropriate male role model. You deserve a medal—and a vacation. You are extraordinary, but you should not have to be both a mother and a father to your children. It is primarily a man's job to show a boy how to be a responsible man and to give daughters a sense of security and safety because of the men in their lives.

## the father's blessing

Let me say something that may cause a measure of angst for some of you. Listen to me very carefully: There is a principle that says you cannot give what you do not have. We talked earlier about the power and significance of the spoken blessing. Some of you have never received any kind of spoken blessing from your parents, and most significantly from your father, whether formal or informal.

Some of you may not even know your father. Many of you know only words of cursing and harsh criticism from a father or mother or both. You know that hole in your heart that has never been filled because you have never received your father's blessing. The analogy Chuck Stecker uses is a checking account with no deposits in the account. You may have checks to write, but you have no deposits to draw upon. You have an empty blessing account in your own life.

You need to know that deposits can be made to your account so you can pass them onto another generation, even if your father is no longer alive or able to make such a deposit in your life. If you are going to be an unclogged pipeline of God's blessing and grace in the lives of your children and grandchildren, it is essential that you have the *good word* deposited into your life in order to deposit into another's.

Though I am speaking primarily to men in this chapter, I want men and women to know that no matter your situation, there are men in your life who can deposit a father's blessing to fill that hole in your own heart. I urge you to seek them out. Find a wise, godly, trusted friend who will make that deposit for you. Even more importantly, remember that our heavenly Father has more than sufficient deposits waiting to be made into your account. The first deposit was made the moment you became His adopted child in Christ. May God show you how much you are valued and treasured, and may He fill your blessing account to overflowing as a constant source of blessing to your children and grandchildren.

## a holy dare

The apostle Paul wrote to the church at Philippi with these words, *"Whatever you have learned or received or heard from me, or seen in me—put into practice."* That's an amazing statement to make. *It's almost like a dare. I dare you to find something in my life not worth imitating.* Would you say to your grandchildren, "Follow my example. Everything I say and do is how you should also live"? That's a pretty courageous and radical thing to say. But that exactly what Paul is saying. *"Put into practice,"* he says, **"everything** *you see in me"* (see Philippians 4:9, emphasis mine).

Is it realistic to live that kind of life? Not only is it realistic, it is imperative if we are going to show the next generations God's goodness, greatness, and glory. It is possible because of God's divine power through which we are partakers of Christ's life in us. Will we make mistakes? Without a doubt. But even those mistakes ought to be an example of how to demonstrate a fully mature life in Christ characterized by humility expressed through confession and forgiveness.

Now, more than ever, our children need heroes, especially male heroes, who serve as examples of what it means to be a godly, fully mature man. Who will step to the plate?

It's time to stop the cycle of irresponsibility. Grandfathers, you can make it right. Take your role seriously, and you will make a difference in your grandsons' lives. Do not abdicate this responsibility and hope someone else will step in the gap.

Even if your sons and sons-in-law are doing a great job, don't be a deadbeat grandfather. Get on your knees right now and ask God to show you how you can reinforce the process or supply what is missing. God will never ask you to do what He has not already equipped you to do.

A famous poem written by John Maxwell Edmonds has memorialized those who gave their lives fighting the enemies of our land. The last two lines of that poem read:

> *When you go home, Tell them of us and say,*
> *For your tomorrow, We gave our today.*[2]

Our sons and grandsons, daughters and granddaughters need men who give themselves so that they can have a tomorrow filled with hope and a capital 'L' Life. These are the next generations of husbands and fathers, wives and mothers. What kind of legacy will we leave to them to build upon for another generation?

## find us faithful

The movie, *Courageous*, a Christian film produced by Sherwood Pictures, is a powerful story about responsible manhood. In the midst of tragedy and uncertainty, four men resolve to be the best fathers and husbands they can be according to God's plan. Out of one man's study and commitment, a Father's Resolution was developed and presented in a solemn ceremony with their families. They pledged to hold each other accountable to the terms of this resolution.

I encourage every grandfather to also adopt this resolution. I urge you to find a band of grand-brothers who will stand with you in a pledge of accountability. Purchase a copy of *The Resolution for Men Study Guide*. In it you will find the Resolution and an opportunity to dig deep into what it means and how it impacts the way we live our lives. Use it as a framework for accountability with your band of courageous grand-brothers. Be proactive—join the cause.

If there's a song that ought to be a Grandparent's Anthem across this land, it is John Mohr's song, *Find Us Faithful*. For me John's moving song, powerfully recorded by Steve Green, captures the essence of courageous, radical grandparenting in a broken world like ours. The chorus of John's song sums it all up:

> *Oh may all who come behind us find us faithful*
> *May the fire of our devotion light their way.*
> *May the footprints that we leave*
> *Lead them to believe,*
> *And the lives we live inspire them to obey.*
> *Oh may all who come behind us find us faithful.*[3]

May the generations that follow behind us find us faithful. When asked who their heroes are, may your courageous faithfulness cause your children and grandchildren to emphatically declare, **you are!** What does it mean to be found faithful? It means to…

- **Wake up** to the reality that a generation—our grandchildren's generation—could grow up not knowing the Lord if we don't repent for our sins and ask God to use us to reclaim the hearts for His kingdom;

- **Wise up** to the world our grandchildren must navigate and learn what to do to avoid the traps the enemy has set for them;

- **Rise up** and embrace the purposes God has for us as His workmanship, investing our assets for His purposes;

- **Build up** those in our family, and outside our family, with words of blessing and the Word of life;

- **Sign up** as soldiers in the cause to fight for the hearts and souls of our children and grandchildren. If you are serious about staying in the race and working to build a movement of godly, intentional grandparents, here are five things you can do:

  1. **Keep in touch!** Sign up for my free weekly email newsletter and blog called *Not On My Watch!* I'll share with you helpful tips and resources to assist you in your personal and community effort to build this movement in your sphere of influence.

  2. **Share the cause with lots of people.** You are the best source of spreading the word. If you agree that the souls of our children and grandchildren are at risk, and this book has been helpful, then order more copies to share with your friends. Go to our web site at www. gocgn.org/bookstore to order additional copies.

  To help you get the word out to your group or church, here's what I would like to do. If you order 350 copies of my book, *Courageous Grandparenting,* I'll come anywhere in the US or Canada for a weekend to do a seminar, speak to groups in your church, and consult with your staff and leaders in your church for FREE. I'll give you a 20% discount off the retail price of the book, and I'll even pay all my own expenses. Consider these few valuable ways you could put this offer to work for you:

· Give the books as a way to generate enthusiasm for a special church event or outreach;
· Use it as an incentive to sign people up for a *Courageous Grandparenting* conference in your church or city;
· Use it as a premium for a worthy fundraising event;
· It would make a great gift to give to grandparents on Grandparents' Day.

3. **Organize a *Courageous Grandparenting* small group study in your church or neighborhood**. Invite other grandparents to join you to learn how to be intentional grandparents.

4. **Participate in the national Grandparent's Day of Prayer event each September**. Use this event to launch ongoing Grandparents at Prayer (G@P) groups to regularly to pray for each your grandchildren, families, schools and each other.

5. **Organize a band of concerned men and women to develop a rites of passage tradition in the church and family**. We must take seriously the responsibility of the family to disciple our children from childhood to adulthood and then on to full maturity in Christ. Chuck Stecker and *A Chosen Generation* can help you do that. Consider investing three days with Chuck to bring the *Men of Honor, Women of Virtue Conference* to your church or community. Visit www. achosengeneration.info to find out more.

Courageous grandparents seek to build and live a lasting legacy of faith for the next generations. It is the legacy of heroes who live poured out, planned out, and prayed out for those coming after. May all who come behind us find us faithful—to the praise of His glory and for the salvation of all who will come after. Amen and amen!

# food for thought and discussion:

Read Philippians 4:9 and Titus 2:1-8.

- Is there anything not covered by Paul's list of what others should imitate in him? How realistic is Paul's statement? Would you be able to say such a thing to your grandchildren? Why or why not?

- Why is the role of a father or grandfather so important in a child's life and development? What lies have we bought into that have led to so many fatherless homes today?

- What impact or influence has your father had in your life (positive or negative)? Have you ever received your father's blessing? What does God expect of you as a father and grandfather (mother and grandmother)? How well are you living up to that expectation? What would your spouse or children say?

- What are ways you can actively be involved in "teaching" the younger generations what it means to move from childhood to adulthood?

# action steps:

- If you have never received your father's blessing, share what that means to you. Is there is something in your own relationship with your father that you need to forgive? Are you willing to take the necessary steps towards that forgiveness? Ask the group to pray with you about a godly man who can make that deposit into your blessing account. Perhaps there is someone in your group who can fill that role.

- Talk together about ways to implement a rites of passage tradition and ceremony for the children/grandchildren in your lives. Talk to your church leaders about helping you to implement that plan. Give them a copy of Stecker's book, *Men of Honor/Women of Virtue*.

Men, consider finding a time to meet together as a band of 'grand-brothers' to explore the Resolution study together. Consider inviting a few other 'grand-brothers' to join you.

# chapter notes

**Preface**

1. *You Lost Me*, David Kinnaman, Barna Group-Baker Books, 2011, Kindle Books Loc. 485.

2. *Don't Waste Your Life*, Dr. John Piper, Crossway Books, 2003, pgs. 32-33.

**Chapter 1**

1. *Only One Life*, a poem written by C.T. Stubbs, missionary to China, India and finally the African Congo, where he died at the age of seventy. He founded the Heart Of Africa Mission, which later became known as WEC (World Evangelism Crusade) International. These familiar lines from his poem are just to lines from each stanza or verse of the original poem, which begins as follows:

> *Two little lines I heard one day*
> *Traveling along life's busy way,*
> *Bringing conviction to my heart*
> *And from my mind would not depart;*
> *Only one life twill soon be past,*
> *Only what's done for Christ will last.*

**Chapter 2**

1. Connie Cass and Stacy A. Anderson, "When Can You Call Someone Old? Just Ask A Boomer", The Associated Press, July 17, 2011 issue of The Gazette.

2. "Grandparenting Statistics In the US", www.grandparentsmagazine.net/gpstatistics.htm

3. eds., "Surprising Facts About Grandparents", grandparents.com, August 12, 2009

4. loc.cit, grandparents.com

5. loc. cit, "Grandparenting Statistics"

6. AARP 2002 Survey, http://assets.**aarp**.org/rgcenter/general/gp_2002.pdf

7. AARP 2002 survey

8. Thomas Friedman, a liberal columnist with the *New York Times*, made an interesting observation in an article he wrote entitled, *The Clash Of The Generations*, July 16. 2011. In the article he makes the case that the generations that "came of age in the last 50 years will be remembered

most for the incredible bounty and freedom it received from its parents and the incredible debt burden and constraints it left on its kids." This is the generation Tom Brokaw called the *Great Generation*.

## Chapter 3

*Ruth Nemzoff has written a valuable book about building rewarding relationships with your adults children entitled, *Don't Bite Your Tongue: How To Foster Rewarding Relationships With Your Adult Children*. While not written from a biblical or Christian perspective, she provides wonderful anecdotes and insights into managing a positive relationship without a trite one-size-fits-all approach that many writers take. It provides a very helpful perspective for grandparents.

Another very helpful book for those dealing with extremely difficult situations because of painful choices their adult children make is Allison Bottke's book, *Setting Boundaries With Your Adult Children*. A publication of Harvest House, Allison writes from a biblical point of view about tough love issues. If you are engaged in heart-wrenching situations with your adult children, you should consider reading this book.

## Chapter 4

* Compiled from various accounts of Dr. Hendricks life, including an articles in the March issue of DTS Magazine after his memorial service, and books authored by Dr. Hendricks in which he told his story of his childhood.

## Chapter 5

1. *The Meaning Of Marriage: Facing The Complexities of Commitment With The Wisdom of God*, by Timothy Keller, founding pastor of Redeemer Presbyterian Church in New York City; 2011.

Americans have not taken divorce seriously, especially as it impacts our children caught in the web of divorce. Here are some *Shocking Statistics About Children and Divorce* by Larry Bilotta, Marriage Success Secrets, www.marriage-success-secrets.com; various sources are cited in this blog for each of the statistics listed. See his web site for the sources. These are things our adult children need to know, and we need to be discussing with our teen grandchildren as they begin thinking about opposite sex relationships in dating and marriage.

Consider some samplings of the damage caused to our children by the divorce-as-a-way-of-life mentality in our society:

- Half of all American children will witness the breakup of a parent's marriage. Of these, nearly half will also see the breakup of a parent's second marriage.

- Forty percent of children growing up in America are being raised without their father.

- Studies in the early 1980s show that children in repeat divorces earned lower grades and their peers rated them as less pleasant to be around.

- Compared to children from homes disrupted by death, children from divorced homes have more psychological problems.

- Children living with both biological parents are 20-35 percent more physically healthy than other children from broken homes.

- Seventy percent of long-term prison inmates grew up in broken homes.

- Children and adults from broken homes are nearly twice as likely to attempt suicide than those who do not come from broken homes.

2. *The State of Our Unions* monitors the current health of marriage and family life in America. Produced annually, it is a joint publication of the National Marriage Project at the University of Virginia and the Center for Marriage and Families at the Institute for American Values; editor: W. Bradford Wilcox; www.stateofourunions.org.

The *2011 State of Our Unions* explores the links between marriage, parenthood, meaning in life, and happiness; it also identifies ten factors that are associated with high levels of marital happiness among married parents. The articles cited in this writing are from the section entitled Social Indicators of Marital Health and Wellbeing: Marriage, Divorce, Unmarried Cohabitation, Loss of Child Centeredness, Fragile Families with Children, Teen Attitudes about Marriage and Family.

3. "Defining Marriage Down", by Adam Mersereau, Touchstone: A Journal of Mere Christianity; November 2003

**Note:** The subject of same-sex marriage is gaining speed in our country, and if allowed to continue as it is, it will have devastating repercussion upon the traditional family in America. It behooves us all to equip ourselves well for the discussions (if permitted) that will need to be engaged. T. M. Moore and the Colson Center have prepared some very useful and information resources and activities for engaging in this conversation. I have listed these in the Appendix. I urge you to read up, wise up and be proactive about seeking opportunities to compassionately and graciously engage in dialogue with your families and grandchildren.

4. "I'm Gay and I Oppose Same-Sex Marriage", by Doug Mainwaring, *Public Discourse*, March 8, 2013.

## Chapter 6
1. Holly Catterton Allen and Christine Lawton Ross, *Intergenerational Christian Formation: Bringing the Whole Church Together in Ministry, Community and Worship*, IVP Academic, 2012, Kindle ebook loc. 379.
2. *One Woman's 'Truth': Reille Hunter Talks to Oprah*; Alessandra Stanley, New York Times, April 30, 2010.
3. *Abortion and the Moral Conscience of a Nation* by Ronald Reagan (New Regency Publishing), 2010, pg. 4.
4. Speech at Lewistown, Illinois, August 17, 1858. While speaking of slavery and the tyranny of governments, he was drawing on an eternal principles that apply to all of human life.
5. Mother Teresa, *My Life for the Poor*, San Francisco (Harper SanFrancisco), 2005.
6. *More Americans Tailoring Religion to Fit Their Needs*, by Cathy Lynn Grossman, USA Today, September 14, 2011.
7. *All That Jesus Asks* by Stan Guthrie, 2010 (Baker Books), pg. 46.

## Chapter 7
1. *Place and Placelessness in America: The New Meaning of Mobility*; Christine Rosen, The New Atlantis: A Journal of Technology and Society, Number 31, Spring 2011, pp. 40-46.

2. *God's Technology: Training Our Children to Use Technology to God's Glory*, Dr. David Murray, www.HeadHeartHand.org, Puritan Reformed Theological Seminary. A free study guide is available with the DVD.

## Chapter 8
1. *Amusing Ourselves to Death: Public Discourse in the Age of Show Business*, Neil Postman, Penguin Books, 1985, pg.xix.

2. Lamplighter Daily Moments, *Amusing Ourselves to Death* by Mark Hamby, October 5, 2010; Lamplighter Publishing, www.lamplighterpublishing.com.
3. *Growing Up Digital—Wired for Distraction*; Matt Richtel, The New York Times, November 21, 2010.
4. *Amusing Ourselves to Death: Public Discourse in the Age of Show Business*, Neil Postman, Penguin Books, 1985, pg.xx.
5. *Is True Friendship Dying Away?*, Mark Vernon, USA Today, July 26, 2010.
6. *Generation M²: Media In The Lives of 8- To 18-Year-Olds*; A Kaiser Family Foundation Study, January 2010.
7. *Myth: A Little TV Never Hurt Anybody*, Bill Bumpus, OneNewsNow article based upon an interview with Melissa Henson of the Parents Television Council, May 5, 2010; Research data from a study published in the *Archives of Pediatrics and Adolescent Medicine*.
8. *Predator Statistics*, InternetSafety101.org web site, Enough Is Enough, a ministry of Youth For Christ to make the internet safer for children and families; research data provided by the Crimes Against Children Research Center. A great deal of valuable information is available through the Enough Is Enough web site that would useful to both parents and grandparents. www.enough.org or www.internetsafety101.org.

## Chapter 10

1. *Dual Commissions: Evangelizing and Engaging Culture*, Chuck Colson, Breakpoint, November 30, 2011. www.colsoncenter.org
2. op. cit., *Dual Commissions*
3. *Culture Making: Recovering Our Creative Calling*, Andy Crouch, IVP Books, 2009.
4. Ibid., pg. 69.

## Chapter 11

1. *Don't Waste Your Life,* John Piper, Crossway Books, Wheaton, IL, 2003, page 32. One of Piper's best books on practical Christian living. The big idea of this book is living lives that display the glory and greatness of God in all we do. It involves risk, suffering, mission, mercy and joy because Christ is our treasure.

Because RAD grandparenting is about taking risk and self-denial, Piper's teaching from God's Word is right on the money for grandparents who take their roles seriously and do not buy into the retirement myth. And as John Piper notes, risk taking involves living our lives in such a way that we "show he [Jesus] is more precious than life…if we walk away from risk to keep ourselves safe and solvent, we will waste our lives". This is a book every grandparent (and every believer) should read. Piper's perspective on new

birth and the resultant life that makes Christ look great—that He is our "all-satisfying treasure"—is at the heart of the Gospel and what it means to not waste our lives. If we do, an entire generation could grow up not knowing the Lord and truth that can set them free to be all God created us to be.
2. *Ibid.*, pg. 10.

## Chapter 12

1. *The Ultimate Gift*, Jim Stovall, David C. Cook, Colorado Springs, CO, 2001, pgs. 146 and 151.

> Also available in a movie version. Either the book or the movie would be an excellent resource to use with your grandchildren followed by a discussion about those things in life that really matter. A study guide is also available to work through with your children/grandchildren. For more information about this book, DVD and other resources, visit the web site at www.theultimategift.com.

2. *How Should We Then Live? The Rise and Decline of Western Thought and Culture*, Francis Schaeffer, Crossway Books, Wheaton, IL, 1976.

> Francis Schaeffer, theologian, author, philosopher, pastor and found of L'Abri communties in Switzerland, wrote a number of works dealing with cultural issues and the arts with the eye of a Christian apologists. His two major works were *A Christian Manifesto* and *What Ever Happened To The Human Race* (also a film series) dealt with the problem of secular humanism in which man is the measure of all things, not God and the Word. Another of his works, also made into a film documentary, was *How Should We Then Live? The Rise and Decline of Western Thought and Culture*. In this work he traces western history from the time of ancient Rome to the mid-1970's and the changing patterns of thought the developed throughout these periods. He warned of the destructive consequences of building a society on humanism, which ultimately produces relativism and no way to distinguish right from wrong. He purpose was to challenge society to consider the ultimate consequences of basing a society on humanism rather than the absolute truth of God's Word and an infinite, personal God. He foresaw the cultural changes that now pervade our time. While his warnings were greatly discussed in churches and student groups across the land, his warnings still went largely unheeded.

## Chapter 13

1. *The Treasure Principle*, by Randy Alcorn; pg. 19-20. Randy unpacks the secret of giving according to the radical teaching of Jesus. This little books

is full of powerful truths that will change your life and the lives of your children/grandchildren if your embrace them.

2. Piper, *op. cit.,* page 72.

## Chapter 14

1. *The Blessing*, Gary Smalley and John Trent, Ph.D., Thomas Nelson Publishers, Nashville, TN, 1986, pg. 24.

> This is a read for every grandparent who wants to be a conduit of blessing in their family's life. Written in 1986 it is filled with practical tools and applications for establishing an environment of blessing in the home. We would do well to take to heart the teaching and practical suggestions offered in this book.

2. *Inappropriate touch*: Because touch is so central to our relationship, inappropriate touch is an abomination. It can irreparably devastate a life and relationship. True, the paranoia and fear that hangs over us should our touch be misunderstood can hinder us from reaching out appropriately. I understand the care we must exercise because of the profusion of perverts in our society. However, as is often the case, our overreactions have unleashed a new monster that seeks to hinder, if not dismantle, the relational needs we all have as image-bearers of God.

The No Touch Monster is fed by suspicion and paranoia. Tragically, our physical withdrawals due to our fear that the No Touch Monster may be paroling around looking for someone to devour, only deprives another of that which is desperately needed. We must be wise and sensitive, but not paranoid. How do we discern the difference between appropriate and inappropriate touch?

We start by taking a good look at ourselves. Appropriate, meaningful touch is motivated by a desire to bless someone with the most effective means possible. It is not concerned with the feelings of the one giving the blessing. The person who is looking for a pleasurable experience is walking down a dangerous, destructive path. If it is ever about you, it will probably be inappropriate. This requires some honest self-examination. We also need to make ourselves accountable to others. It is not hard to pick up on red flags in those who are disingenuous.

Appropriate touch, on the other hand (no pun intended), can be something as simple as a hand on the shoulder or head, or even a gentle touch on the arm. In the right situations a hug or a kiss may be appropriate expressions of love and value. Always ask, *Will this be meaningful and provide the most positive response possible for the one I wish to bless? How will the person I want to bless most likely respond to this expression of love and affection?*

Careless expressions of touch rooted in self-gratifying motivations turn an opportunity to bless into a curse, even if it was unintentional. Our responsibility is to guard our heart and make sure we know what is appropriate in any situation. The way in which we reach out to a small child might not be appropriate for a young teen, especially someone of the opposite sex. How a man reaches out to a young woman, even if she is a granddaughter, may be very different from how another woman may embrace that same young woman.

## Chapter 16
1. *Well-Versed Living* by Caroline Boykin; *Significant Living*, September 2011 issue.
2. *The Well-Versed Family: Raising Kids of Faith Through (Do-Able!) Scripture Memory* by Caroline Boykin, Tate Publishing, 2007, web site: www.wellversedliving.com.
3. *Passing On A Written Legacy* by Lana Rockwell. Lana provides some very practical ways to recall much of your life story and write it down so that your family will have a first person perspective on the family history. Web site: www.mymemoriesforyou.net

## Chapter 17
1. *The Spiral of Silence: Public Opinion—Our Social Skin*, Elisabeth Noelle-Neumann, 1993, University of Chicago Press.

> The spiral of silence is the theory that a person is less likely to voice an opinion on a topic if one feels that one is in the minority for fear of reprisal or isolation from the majority. It begins with fear of reprisal or isolation, and escalates from there. The fear of isolation is the centrifugal force that accelerates the spiral of silence. Noelle-Neuman suggests demonstrates how mass media play a large part in determining what the dominant opinion is due to the fact that our direct observation of issues is limited to a small percentage of the population. The mass media have an enormous impact on how public opinion is portrayed, and can dramatically impact an individual's perception about where public opinion lies, whether or not that portrayal is factual. Noelle-Neumann describes the spiral of silence as a dynamic process, in which predictions about public opinion become

**fact** as mass media's coverage of the minority opinion becomes the status quo, and the majority becomes less likely to speak out. We see this carried out in the political correct arenas of morality and social justice. Intimidation, when a minority opinion is imposed upon a larger majority through fear of reprisal or unmerited accusations, becomes a primary means of silencing the majority opinion and compelling it to adopt what it might otherwise reject.

### Crucial points to the theory

- People have a fear of being rejected by those in their social environment, which is called "fear of isolation."

- People are constantly observing the behaviors of those around them, and seeing which gain approval and disapproval from society.

- People unconsciously issue their own threats of isolation by showing signals of approval or disapproval.

- Threats of isolation are avoided by a person's tendency to refrain from making a statement about something they think might attract objections.

- People are more willing to publicly state things that they believe will be accepted positively.

- The spiral effect begins because when people who are seen as representing majority opinion, often authority figures, speak out confidently. The opposition feels a greater sense of fear of isolation and is further convinced to remain silent, since they perceive themselves to be in the minority. The feelings continue to grow in either direction exponentially.

- A strong moral component is necessary for the issue to activate the spiral.

- If there is a social consensus, the spiral will not be activated. There must be two opposing forces.

- The mass media has a strong influence on this process.

- Fear and threat of isolation are subconscious processes.

- The spiral of silence only "holds a sway" over the public for a limited time.

- If a topic activates the spiral of silence, this means that the issue is a great threat to social cohesion.

2. *The False Enforcement of Unpopular Norms*, Willer, Kuwabara, and Macy, University of California, Berkeley.

An informative study in the reasons and influences behind the enforcement of group consensus and unpopular norms that violate individual private beliefs. Jim Jones and the Jonestown Massacre is one example of how masses can be persuaded and convinced by charismatic leaders to do the most extreme actions and adopt extreme beliefs not otherwise held. In fact, not only do individuals comply to such extreme norms, but they enforce others to do so as well. The study suggests that people become trapped in a "self-enforcing equilibrium in which they pressure one another in order to cover up their own private doubts", and this may appear genuine to casual observers and even researchers if they do not understand the reality of "false enforcement".

## Chapter 18

1. *Grandparenting with a Purpose: Effective Ways to Pray for Your Grandchildren*, Lillian Ann Penner, Crossbooks, A Division of Lifeway, 2010. Copies can also be orderd from Christian Grandparenting Network at www.christiangrandparenting.net.

2. The Manhattan Declaration was written by a group of prominent Christian clergy, ministry leaders, and scholars and released publicly on November 20, 2009 at a press conference in Washington, DC. The 4,700-word declaration speaks in defense of the sanctity of life, traditional marriage, and religious liberty. It issues a clarion call to Christians to adhere firmly to their convictions in these three areas. A complete copy of the text, and an opportunity to join the thousands who have signed the document, can be found at www.manhattandeclaration.org.

3. Dr. Martin Luther, Jr. , *Letter From Birmingham Jail,* April 16, 1963. Written while confined to the Birmingham city jail following a civil rights demonstration in that city.

4. DVD: *Do The Right Thing: A Six-Part Exploration of Ethics*, hosted by Chuck Colson and Robert George, Colson Center for Christian Worldview and The Witherspoon Institute. Visit www.doingtherightthing.com for more information.

5. Dr. Mark Young, "Charitable Orthodoxy", Denver Seminary Magazine, Summer 2011, pg. 2.

## Chapter 19

1. *Reviving Fatherhood*, Viewpoint by Mark Earley, January 14, 2010, www.breakpoint.org

2. The Kohima Epitaph, The Burma Star Association, www.burmastar. org.uk. The text of these words used on several war memorials come from a poem written by John Maxwell Edmonds (1875 -1958), an English Classicist, who had put them together among a collection of 12 epitaphs for WWI in 1916.

3. *Find Us Faithful*, music and lyrics by John Mohr, 1987; copyright Gaither Music Company, 1703 S Park AvenueAlexandria, IN 46001-8063. Used by permission.

# appendix 1
## technology resources

1. *Flickering Pixels: How Technology Shapes Your Faith*, Shane Hipps, Zondervan Publishing, 2009.

2. Heidi Jusczak, "Facebook Faux Pas: The Secret Code of Social Networking with Your Grandkids", Grand Magazine, Sept/Oct. 2011 issue. *www.grandmagazine.com*

3. Tricia Goyer, "Parents in a Digital World", Parent Edition of April 2007 issue of Focus on the Family magazine. Available online at *www.focusonthefamily.com/parenting*

4. *Character in a Tech-Overloaded World*, by Linda Keffer, Helping Families Thrive web site at Focus on the Family. Available online at *www.focusonthefamily.com/parenting*

5. Christine Rosen, "Virtual Friendship and the New Narcissim", The New Atlantis, Number 17, Summer 2007, pp. 15-31. You can find the article online at *www.thenewatlantis.com/publications/virutal-friendship-and-the-new-narcissim*.

6. *Plugged In (www.pluggedin.com)*; an online publication of Focus On The Family designed to shine a light on the world of popular entertainment while giving families the essential tools they need to understand, navigate and impact the culture in which they live. Through reviews, articles and discussions, the goal is to "spark intellectual thought, spiritual growth and a desire to follow the command of Colossians 2:8: 'See to it that no one takes you captive through hollow and deceptive philosophy, which depends on human tradition and the basic principles of this world rather than on Christ.'" This is a valuable resource for families in a number of media technology arenas, including movies, video games, TV, music, etc.

7. *Pew Internet (www.pewinternet.org)*; a project of the Pew Research Center; a nonpartisan, nonprofit "fact tank" that provides information on the issues, attitudes and trends shaping America and the world. The Project produces reports exploring the impact of the internet on families, communities, work and home, daily life, etc. Web site:

8. *Wired Safety (www.wiredsafety.org)*; provides one-to-one help, extensive resources, information, and education to people of all ages on a myriad of Internet, mobile, gaming and interactive technology safety issues. Web site:

9. *Common Sense Media (www.commonsense.org)*; Common Sense Media is dedicated to improving the lives of kids and families by providing the trustworthy information, education, and independent voice they need to thrive in a world of media and technology.

# plan a tech-fast

As with all the good things, there are downsides as well. In spite of the benefits we enjoy with all the technology available to us today, diligence will increase our awareness of the threat technology can make to authentic human relationships. We can be in the same room together, and still be completely isolated from one another. Obsessions with social networking, texting, online games, and the growing use of portable devices like smartphones, tablets, and mobile game devices, make it easy to avoid relationship engagement in meaningful conversations.

At the same time, technology has increased our ability to connect with people anywhere in the world like never before. This is a huge benefit for those wanting to stay connected even though we are separated by long distances. The convenience of cell phone connectivity has made some aspects of life better and safer. Unfortunately the flip-side of this great blessing is what I call *technobesity*. We are growing fat, relationally disconnected, and overloaded with useless information in the world of cyberspace. What can we do to counter this trend toward technobesity?

I suggest we try a 'tech-fast' for a period. A food fast from time to time helps to cleanse our physical bodies of toxins. When combined with prayer, it is a spiritual cleansing as well. So, why not do a 'tech-fast' from time to time? It can be for a day, two days, a week, or whatever period of time you choose. You could declare a 'tech-fast' for just a few hours when family comes to visit.

Here are some suggestions to make your tech-fast profitable and beneficial for all. If you just can't do it all, then you may have a serious case of technobesity that may warrant some more drastic measures. F. B. Meyer wrote, "We never test the resources of God until we attempt the impossible." At a time when our lives are consumed with technology, it might seem like an impossible task. Just give it a try. Here are some ideas for implementing a tech-fast. See if it doesn't make a difference in your own family.

> 1. Sit down with family members and discuss the idea. Why are you doing it? What do you hope to accomplish? What are the benefits? How long will the fast period be? If you get the nod to move ahead, work together to plan how the time will be spent. (Remember, if you just fast

from technology, but plan nothing to substitute for it, you are really planning to fail.)

2. Agree to turn off and NOT USE your TV, iPhone (or Smartphone), iPad, tablets or computers. No iPods or mp3 players allowed. That means you will not be checking email or Facebook or Twitter during the period of the fast.

3. Here are some ways to use your time during the tech-fast:
      a. Pray
      b. Sit down and talk. Talk about life experiences currently going on, social issues, or family history. Ask questions that require more than 'yes' or 'no' answers.
      c. Play some table games
      d. Talk a walk or go to the park and toss a frisby or ball
      e. Do a Bible study together.
4. Conclude the tech-fast period by speaking a personal blessing over each member of your family—spouse, grandchildren, children, etc.

5. Debrief: briefly evaluate what you experienced. What did your learn? What were the challenges? Can you do it again? What would you do differently?

Author's Note: I'd like to hear from you about your personal experience with doing a tech-fast. Send me an email at *charper@christiangrandparenting.net* and tell me how it went.

*One more thought*: consider a limited fast in which all cell phones, computers, game devices, iPods and television programs are off-limits, but allow watching a selected movie (like *Courageous* or *October Baby*), or a teaching DVD (such as *Doing the Right Thing*) followed by an interaction time with your family or friends.

# appendix 2
## living will worksheets

### asset inventory
### disposition worksheet

All the Living Living Will worksheets are available as downloads from our web site at **www.christiangrandparenting.net/resources/downloads**. As you sit down with pen and paper, you will discover assets that you never thought about. I encourage you to simply start writing and see what flows. The act of writing will stimulate your memory to recall things you might have all but forgotten. In fact, if your spouse is available, you may find it valuable to work on this together. Two heads really can be better for stimulating memory recall.

Two things you need to keep in mind as you work on this asset list. First, this list is not a way to boost your ego by calling attention to the wonderful person you are and focusing the spotlight on yourself. We all like to receive strokes from others; that's natural, Just remember that God opposes pride— not exactly the best position to be in. It is good to receive affirmation of the gifts and assets God has given to us, but we also need to guard our hearts in the process. The only boasting we should be doing is in our Lord who is the Giver of all good gifts.

Second, don't think of this as a *bucket list*. In other words, this is not an attempt to put together a list of things *you* always wanted to do before you kick the bucket. Think of this as an inventory of what God has given you to invest or spend for someone else according to His purposes for your life and theirs. What you will discover as you do that is how fun and exciting this adventure is and how much it fulfills your deepest desires more than any self-focused bucket list could do. Remember that humility is more than *not* thinking too highly of yourself. It also means not under-estimating who you are and what God has given you. That does not give God glory either. These assets did not originate with you—they were given to you by God. Celebrate what you have been given, but always making much of Christ, not you.

One more thing—as you prepare your asset inventory, give careful thought and prayer to the 'beneficiaries' God is preparing for these assets. Who does God want you to bless with each designated asset? What difference could this mean for that person's (or persons') life? Ask God to reveal the obvious and not so obvious assets that He wants you to dispose in a way that blesses and leads others towards full maturity in Christ. Ask for wisdom to confirm the who, what, why, and how.

Remember, that these assets are related to God's calling and glory uniquely displayed through you as His image-bearer. That glory will be revealed through your obedience. Be prepared for opposition and frustration along the way, but enjoy the adventure and the amazing work God will do in you along the way. Before you start, I encourage you to work through the *14-Day Spiritual Adventure* in Appendix 3.

# appendix 3
## 14 day spiritual journey

### preparing to implement
### the *living* livingwill plan

This 14-day spiritual journey is an adventure in trust and faith. You are choosing to act upon God's promises in response to His commands to bless others with the various assets He has given you. This is not necessarily a comfortable or easy journey to take. If you have to tight a hold on that which you have, material or otherwise, or if you have trouble acknowledging how much God has given to you for His purposes, you will find this journey difficult, if not impossible, to continue. On the other hand, if you persevere by faith, I believe you will see God work in ways you may never have dreamed possible.

Remember Jesus' words that your life does not consist in "the abundance of your possessions" (Luke 12:13-21), and that he who would "whoever loses his life for my sake will find it" (Matthew 10:37-39). Proverbs 11:25 describes the generous man, not only as one who prospers, but who is himself refreshed as he refreshes others. The life lived well is a generous and fulfilling life. My prayer is that you will discover the joy of this truth through this spiritual journey. May you not only discover the joy and freedom of living well according to God's purposes, but may the generations who come behind you, your children and grandchildren, be blessed and desire to experience the same refreshing.

Here are some daily guides from God's Word to keep you focused on the good way where God promises rest for your soul and refreshing for others—especially your family. Meditate on these Scriptures. Let them transform your mind and heart, and serve as a call to action by faith. Let the Spirit of God teach you and work in you for the Father's purposes. In this spirit, then, may "God strengthen you with power through His Spirit in your inner being, so that Christ may dwell in your heart through faith" (Eph. 3:16-17), and may He use you and all that He has given you to bless those He desires to bless through you.

*Let the adventure begin!*

# 14-day spiritual journey plan

### DAY 1:

*Scripture: Matthew 19:16-22*

*Action Point:* If you are a person of means and great wealth, this passage is especially difficult. Generosity is always a matter of the heart. Ask God to search your heart and expose anything that may be hindering you from opening your hand to God's purposes for what He has given you.

### DAY 2:

*Scripture: Jeremiah 9:23-24*

*Action Point:* Once more ask the Lord to reveal any points of pride or unwillingness to surrender all He given for His purposes. Take time today to focus on God's goodness and all that He has done for you so that we will not boast in anything but Him and His grace.

### DAY 3:

*Scripture: Matthew 25:14-15*

*Action Point:* Sit down and make an inventory of all the material assets God has given to you. It may be a lot; it may be a little. The point is to acknowledge what God has provided. When you finish your inventory, thank God for what He has provided and acknowledge His ownership.

### DAY 4:

*Scripture: Acts 3:6*

*Action Point:* Material assets are not all the assets God has given us to spend and dispose of for the blessing of others. Take time today and tomorrow to make an inventory of non-material assets God has blessed you with.

### DAY 5:

*Scripture: Matthew 25: 16-30*

*Action Point:* Look over the inventory of assets God has blessed you with. Now ask Him to give you wisdom to understand how He would have you spend, invest or dispose of these assets to bless others. Ask how these assets could be used to bless others. If you have hoarded these assets for yourself, confess that now. With a repentant heart ask for forgiveness, and then offer them with open hand and heart for His purposes.

**DAY 6:**

*Scripture: Ephesians 2:10*

*Action Point:* God has already prepared you and those who will receive the blessings from your hand. Prayerfully make a list of people (family and others) you know God would want use you to bless with these assets He has given you. Pray over each name on the list and ask God to show you how He wants you to invest in each person.

**DAY 7:**

*Scripture: Colossians 3:17*

*Action Point:* Now that you have identified a list of people the Lord wants you to bless as you spend, invest or otherwise dispose of the assets He has given you, ask Him for clear understanding about how best to do that? There may a situation in which you don't know the answer to who, when or where, only what. Simply wait upon the Lord and ask Him to lead you to the individual or individuals He wants to bless through you and give glory to Him.

**DAY 8:**

*Scriptures: 2 Corinthians 8:12; Mark 12:41-44*

*Action Point:* Continue to ask God for wisdom, courage and alertness to His leading. Guard against doubt or the notion that you have nothing to give. Even if you have little materially, the Lord has given you exactly what is needed to bless others, including your family. The poor widow reminds us that it is not the size of the gift or what kind of gift is offered but the willing, worshiping heart of the giver that God will bless.

**DAY 9:**

*Scripture: I Timothy 6:18-19*

*Action Point:* Continuing praying for the people whom God will be sending to you and identifying to you for blessing and meeting a need. Guard your heart so that you are always cheerfully and happily serving those He sends to you, regardless of how they might respond.

**DAY 10:**

*Scripture: 2 Corinthians 9:8, 11*

*Action Point:* What has God revealed to you thus far about your own heart and the needs of those around you? Are there lessons and blessings you have received you want to thank God for and share with others?

**DAY 11:**

*Scripture: Luke 12:15-21*

*Action Point:* You may have begun to discover some of the rare treasures God has entrusted to you to use for His glory. In contrast to the rich farmer in this parable, what have you learned about what it means to live a life that is rich towards God? How can you truly worship Him and live Life (with a capital 'L')—a life that demonstrates what it means to be rich towards God?

**DAY 12:**

*Scriptures: Matthew 6:19-21; Romans 12:1-8*

*Action Point:* Each day from here on out ask the Lord to show you how He wants you to bless another through the assets He has provided. Thank Him for the special blessings He will reveal to you and through you each day.

**DAY 13:**

*Scripture: Philippians 4:-11-12*

*Action Point:* What have I learned about contentment in these last few weeks? How will my life be different as a result?

**DAY 14:**

*Scripture: 2 Corinthians 5:10*

*Action Point:* In light of God's warning about being judged according to the way your life was lived, how does this impact the way you see your life? What have you learned throughout this 14-Day Adventure with God that may change how you use your assets? How could you share what you have learned with others?

# appendix 4
## the blessing

## I. general blessing

The general or recurring blessing (you may choose to do it daily, weekly or monthly) is a powerful tool for helping our children and grandchildren know, love and follow Christ with their all their heart. Through the laying on of hands and the spoken words of blessing, we become conduits for a consistent, deliberate encounter with God's transforming power and favor, and a wall of protection in which they will experience a sense of security in God.

Here are steps that will help you in the establishment of a Recurring Family Blessing for each of your children/grandchildren...

1. If the children are old enough, explain to them what you want to do with the blessing and why.

2. Hold them or touch them in a sincere and meaningful way when you say the blessing over them, laying one hand on their head as a symbol of your being an instrument through which God blesses.

3. Pick a time and frequency and stick with it. It can be daily, weekly, or whenever you have them over to your house, but the key is consistency.

4. Choose the blessing you will say. It can be the same blessing every time, or you can vary the blessing from time to time. (See examples below)

5. JUST DO IT!!! It is never too late to start, but it is always too soon to delay.

# examples of blessings from scripture

*And the LORD spoke to Moses, saying: "Speak to Aaron and his sons, saying, 'This is the way you shall bless the children of Israel. Say to them: "The LORD bless you and keep you; The LORD make His face shine upon you, And be gracious to you; The LORD lift up His countenance upon you, And give you peace." ' "So they shall put My name on the children of Israel, and I will bless them." Numbers 6:22-27 NKJV*

- As Aaron spoke Your blessing over the people of Israel, so I speak Your blessing over my children/grandchildren today.

  _____, may the Lord bless you and keep you; may the Lord make His face to shine upon you and be gracious unto you; may the Lord always look upon you with favor and give you peace in the name of Jesus Christ our Lord.

- Ephesians 3:17-19

  _____, I pray that you, being rooted and established in love, may have power together with all the saints to grasp how wide and long and high and deep is the love of Christ, and to know this love that surpasses knowledge, that you may be filled to the measure of all the fullness of God, in Jesus' name.

- 2 Thessalonians 2:16-17

  _____, may our Lord Jesus Christ Himself and God the Father, who loved us and by His grace gave us eternal encouragement and good hope, encourage your heart and strengthen you in every good deed and word, in the name of the Father, Son and Holy Spirit.

- Romans 15:13

  _____, may the God of hope fill you with all joy and peace as you trust in Him, so that you may overflow with hope by the power of the Holy Spirit, in the name of the Father, Son and Holy Spirit.

May the Lord bless you with His favor and kindness; may He keep you by His power and strength, and deliver them from all evil; may His face shine upon you with the light of His radiant love; may you delight in the abundant riches of God's amazing grace; may the Lord make His face to smile on you; may He shield your heart and mind with His truth and abiding peace, His perfect peace that passes all understanding.

# II. the personal blessing

Few things can be as powerful and meaningful in your child/grandchild's life than a personal, spoken blessing at specific 'milestones' in their life. The pronouncement of blessing has been a part of family life among God's people from the earliest days. Prayerfully consider what God would have you speak into the life of your children that would encourage them and build them up in Christ, then write it out on the page provided. Make it your own and let it speak truth and life into your child/grandchild. A blessing should include the following...

### 1. An Affirmation of High Value

Communicate to your child/grandchild that they are something special, and that you value them highly. Identify a particular trait you wish to emphasize and express how you value that trait. Word pictures can be a powerful way to express that value.

### 2. A Picture of a Special Future

This is a reflection of how well you know your child/grandchild and the gifts and interests he/she has already developed. The idea is to express an expectation of success and accomplishment, not for worldly gain, but according to that which God has already purposed for them. You are saying, "I believe in you and expect you to succeed in that which God has prepared in advance for you."

### 3. An Active Commitment

It great to speak blessing to our children and grandchildren, but now we must demonstrate our willingness to stand with them and walk them in the journey ahead. Inconsistency and lack of follow through will tend to negate any positive reinforcement you may communicate verbally.

*NOTE: Be brief and to the point. Don't worry about all the details of someone's life or another's example. Capture the essence of what you want to say and say it so they will remember it. Here are some examples to help you write your own.*

# example#1

## a grandparents' blessing for

_____

Born:_____

_____, son of _____, welcome to the family.

Words cannot describe how much your grandmother and I are thrilled about your arrival in our family. We have anticipated this moment with great eagerness, and you have not disappointed us.

Though you came into this world through much hardship and pain, you have been received with much joy and delight! With the same measure of struggle and determination with which you have entered this life, so shall your measure of courage, strength and perseverance be in the service of your Creator, Lord and Savior.

Unlike your namesake, who needed to touch the Master's wounds before he could believe, may you know the blessing and anointing of God in a special way because you walk by faith, not by sight. Your name means 'seeker of truth'. May you be a man who passionately seeks after God and His truth, boldly walking in that truth by faith. As a man of faith, a seeker of truth, you will know the reward and cost of following Christ in a hostile world. With God as your help, you will be strong and courageous, not fearing man, but trusting God with your whole heart.

You are blessed with parents who love you and who love the Lord. They have chosen to build their marriage and family upon the foundation of faith in Jesus Christ as Lord and Savior, a foundation that will not crumble. Learn from their example, heed their instruction, and imitate their faith, for in so much as their love grows and endures for one another and the Lord, so shall this blessing be fulfilled in you. We love you, _____, and we will promise to pray for you, your parents, and your place in God's Kingdom as you grow in wisdom, grace and truth.

WITH ALL OUR LOVE,
_Your Proud and Grateful Grandparents_

# example#2

## a grandparents' blessing for

For Our Grandson

_____

While you were yet in your mother's womb, the blessings had already begun in your Grandma's and my heart.

_____, your presence has brought us all joy as we have watched you grow, taken your first steps, and spoken your first words. Your hurts have been our hurts, and we shared in your laughter.

_____, your accepting Jesus Christ into your heart and life was an answer to daily prayer. Our prayers for you now are for God's watchful care over you. May He protect you during these young years, and may you grow up physically, mentally, and spiritually strong. Whatever you choose to do in life, may you always be God's man, and let the light within you shine before family and other people.

_____, with thanksgiving in our hearts, we are thankful to God for being allowed to be part of your life.

Grandma and Grandpa _____

# appendix 5
## additional resources

## legacy journal

The Legacy Journal is a unique tool for providing a written legacy for future generations. The attractively bound journal makes a perfect gift for your family members. You can also download a pdf file version from our web site.

The Journal is divided into two sections.
Section One guides you through the process of recording your own personal and family history, as well as important responses to fun and informative questions your family would enjoy knowing about you.

Section Two is designed to let you write out your personal reflections and perspectives about specific topics of life. Topics include things like Education and Learning, Work and Career, Money and Material Possessions, Aging, Technology, Marriage and Family, God and Faith, etc. The twenty-three topic suggestions provide ample opportunity to share your thoughts about important areas of life you want to pass on to another generation. This section concludes with pages for you to write out a personal blessing to the person receiving the Journal.

## courageous grandparenting conferences & seminars

*Courageous Grandparenting* Conferences and Seminars. Host a seminar in your church or community or attend a *Courageous Grandparenting* Conferences in a beautiful setting at one of our selected conference facilities. Information about hosting a seminar or an upcoming conference can be found at *www.courageousgrandparenting.com*

### *grandparenting with a purpose:*
*Effective Ways to Pray for Your Grandchildren*
by Lillian Penner.

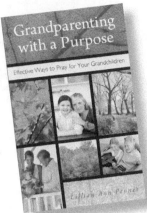

Lillian is the National Prayer Coordinator of the Christian Grandparenting Network. This book will help you develop your prayer life as you pray for your family, and especially your grandchildren. You'll find practical examples of prayer to help you get started, and creative ways to make your prayers more meaningful and effective.

Available at the CGN store: *www.christiangrandparenting.net* or from Lillian's site at *www.grandparentingwithapurpose.com*.

## grandparents' day of prayer

Join with thousands of grandparents across this land each year on the Sunday following Labor Day as we make National Grandparents Day at day of prayer and fasting for our grandchildren, their parents and our nation. Visit our web site at *www. christiangrandparenting. net/day-of-prayer* to find out how you can organize a prayer event in your church or community.

GRANDPARENTS'
DAY OF PRAYER
*Standing in the Gap*

GRANDPARENTS AT PRAYER

## G@P groups

G@P groups meet regularly throughout the year to prayer for each other's grandchildren and families. Join a group or organize one in your area. Click on the G@P icon on our web site to find out more.

## grandcamp programs

Since 1998 the Christian Grandparenting
Network has produced GrandCamps
each summer for grandparents and their
grade-school age grandchildren. Now,
GrandCamps is going national as a
strategic program offering to various
camps, churches and denominations.
A complete GrandCamp curriculum
will be available, along with all
resources needed to host this program in your own church or camp/conference
facility, beginning November 2013. A *Do-It-Yourself* version will also be available
by Spring 2014 for grandparents who would like ideas and resources for doing
their own GrandCamp or Cousins' Camp. Visit www.grandcamps.org for details.

GRANDCAMPS
*Building Lasting Memories & Milestones*

CHRISTIAN
GRANDPARENTING®
N E T W O R K

*Representing Christ to the Next Generations!*

**Christian Grandparenting Network**
www.christiangrandparenting.net
5844 Pioneer Mesa Dr.
Colorado Springs, CO 80923

# 719.522.1404

CPSIA information can be obtained
at www.ICGtesting.com
Printed in the USA
BVHW04s0923090918
526921BV00002B/13/P